IMPACT ASSESSMENT OF

STRESS LEVEL OF WOMEN

Working in 181 Abhayam Women Helpline: A Psycho-Social Analysis

IMPACT ASSESSMENT OF
STRESS LEVEL OF WOMEN

Working in 181 Abhayam Women Helpline: A Psycho-Social Analysis

Dr Neeta Sinha
Ms Simran Bhatia
Ms Riddhima Bhatnagar

KALPAZ

First Published, 2018

Published by

Kalpaz Publications
C-30, Satyawati Nagar,
Delhi – 110052
E-mail: kalpaz@hotmail.com
Ph.: 9212142040

Printed at: G. Print Process, Delhi

Cataloging in Publication Data—DK
Courtesy: D.K. Agencies (P) Ltd. <docinfo@dkagencies.com>

Sinha, Neeta, author.
Impact assessment of stress level of women working in 181 abhayam women helpline : a psycho-social analysis / Dr. Neeta Sinha.
pages cm
Includes bibliographical references.
ISBN 9789386397621 (HB)

1. 181 Abhayam Women Helpline (Gujarat, India).—Employees—Job stress—Evaluation. 2. Women employees—Job stress—India—Gujarat—Evaluation. 3. Helplines—India—Gujarat. 4. Women—Services for—India—Gujarat. I. Title.

HD6190.G85S56 2018 DDC 331.4095475 23

CONTENTS

IMPACT ASSESSMENT OF

STRESS LEVEL OF WOMEN

Working in 181 Abhayam Women Helpline: A Psycho-Social Analysis

2016-2018

IMPACT ASSESSMENT OF STRESS LEVEL OF WOMEN

Working in 181 Abhayam Women Helpline: A Psycho-Social Analysis

ORSP RESEARCH PROJECT

Student Investigators

Riddhima Bhatnagar and Simran Bhatia

Roll No. : 14BLS086 and 14BLS108

Under the guidance of

Dr Neeta Sinha

School of Liberal Studies,

Pandit Deendayal Petroleum University,

Gandhinagar – 382007, Gujarat, INDIA

FOREWORD

Professor (Dr) Nigam Dave
Director,
School of Liberal Studies,
Pandit Deendayal Petroleum University

At the outset I would like to compliment and congratulate the author for such a relevant study. Generally, people who provide counselling or medico-legal help to victims in crisis relentlessly work around the clock with a mission like zeal. However, constant exposure to challenges of the people whom they help, create trauma and stress to them also. 181 Abhayam Women Helpline of Government of Gujarat is an initiative to provide help round the clock to women in distress as one stop solution scheme. It works as referral point during crisis and non-crisis interventions and as such the margin of error on the side of the person handling the helpline is minimal. The author has done an impactful analysis of the factors that cause stress to the women employees who handle the helpline. The study is validated with substantial quantitative sample size and can prove to be a good indicator for improving the system which is already doing well. Author through meticulous study suggests the challenges and solutions. The author deserves all accolades for a socially relevant impact analysis.

PREFACE

Dr Neeta Sinha
Project Guide

The problem of violence and atrocities against women is an important issue relating to women that cannot be ignored. Women in the Indian society have been victims of humiliation, torture and exploitation for as long as we have written records of social organisation and family life. Today, though women are being gradually recognised as important, powerful and meaningful contributors to the life of men; but some of the cruel practices thrive even today.

In spite of the legislative measures adopted in favour of women in our society after Independence, the spread of education and women's gradual economic independence, countless women still continue to be victims of violence and extreme cruelty. Violence against women is a worldwide phenomenon. Although not every woman has experienced it, and many expect not to, fear of violence is an important factor in the lives of most women. Fear of violence is a cause of women's lack of participation in activities beyond the home, as well as inside it. Within the home, women and girls may be subjected to physical and sexual abuse as punishment or as culturally justified assaults. These acts shape their attitude to life, and their expectations of themselves.

Violence against women is on the national agenda. Government is making frantic efforts to find solutions. GVK EMRI in association with Government of Gujarat and Government of Uttar Pradesh established an operating 181 Women Helpline. This 24×7 helpline known as Abhayam in the state of Gujarat is supported by rescue vans with counsellors and lady constable. The free 24×7 helpline, 181, is a toll-free number to support women in distress and is accessible through any mobile or landline. Any woman can access the 181 Abhayam helpline for counselling, guidance, information and also for rescue from various threatening situations including domestic violence.

The type of work that the women helpline workers are doing is commendable. While these helpline workers constantly keep looking into the challenges of women all over, they themselves might be facing a lot of challenges at work. Listening to stressful calls and stories is not everyone's cup of tea. Through this book an attempt has been made to look into the lives of women helpline workers and assess their stress levels. A study was done among the call receivers of women helpline services 181 Abhayam to assess their stress levels. The book incorporates the challenges faced by women workers in 181 emergency services.

ACKNOWLEDGMENTS

The success and final outcome of this project required a lot of guidance and assistance from various people. First of all, we are thankful to GVK EMRI for letting us research on 181 women employees and supporting us throughout the project for a period of one year. We thank Mr. Ashish Dhomse, Partner HR, Mr. Narendra Gohil, Partner, WHL and PPP, and Ms. Samiksha Chauhan, Assistant Partner (HR), GVK EMRI for her help throughout and the women employees for their time and participation which helped us complete the project evenly.

We respect and thank our Director General - Dr Tadisina Kishen Kumar Reddy, Chairman - Standing Committee Shri D. Rajagopalan, IAS (Retd.) and Professor (Dr) Nigam Dave, Director, School of Liberal Studies, for providing us with this opportunity and for giving us support and encouragement to complete the research duly.

We owe our deep gratitude to our project guide Dr Neeta Sinha, who took keen interest in our research and guided us all along, till the completion of it by providing all the necessary information and critical review. We are thankful to Ms Poonam Arora for helping us with Data Analysis and her Qualitative Inputs.

Our gratitude to Office of Research and Sponsored Programmes, PDPU for funding us for this study. We are thankful to and fortunate, to get constant encouragement, support and guidance from all the faculty and staff members of PDPU.

ABOUT UNIVERSITY

Pandit Deendayal Petroleum University's 100 acre campus is located in Gandhinagar, which is the capital city of Gujarat. PDPU offers multiple courses ranging from engineering, arts and management along with maximum exposure and opportunities to its students through various National and International Exchange Programmes and research opportunities with Best Universities worldwide. For development of its faculties and staff the University endeavours for various Joint Exchange and Research programmes.

SCHOOL OF LIBERAL STUDIES

School of Liberal Studies offers Bachelor Honours Degree that equips a student to develop an array of intellectual skills, a variety of methodologies and ways of understanding our changing world, and a broad base of varied knowledge. In turn, such a Liberal Education establishes an invaluable foundation for more specialised study in one's major or in one's profession, for a life-long affinity in learning and intellectual development.

The course imparts classical education in various fields like art, literature, languages, music, dramatics, philosophy, politics, history, law, mathematics, science and general studies. It emphasises on the need to seek knowledge for promoting intellectual growth, creative expression and rational thought.

OFFICE OF RESEARCH AND SPONSORED PROGRAMMES

The Office of Research and Sponsored Programmes provides, to entire PDPU fraternity, support for the free and responsible conduct of investigative, scholarly and creative activities at Pandit Deendayal Petroleum University, Gandhinagar. The Office of Research and Sponsored Programmes offers support from the initial stages of proposal development to grant management, publication and the transfer of technology. It provides internally funded grants, pre-award and post-award support for externally funded grants and offers education and support information on grant compliance and the responsible conduct of research.

STUDENT RESEARCH PROGRAMME

The objective of the Student Research Project Financial Assistance is to carry out research projects by PDPU students. This scheme aims to encourage research and innovation among the PDPU fraternity. A research topic of high quality, originality and relevance is selected out of various proposals and further funded for a year long intensive research by the project investigators.

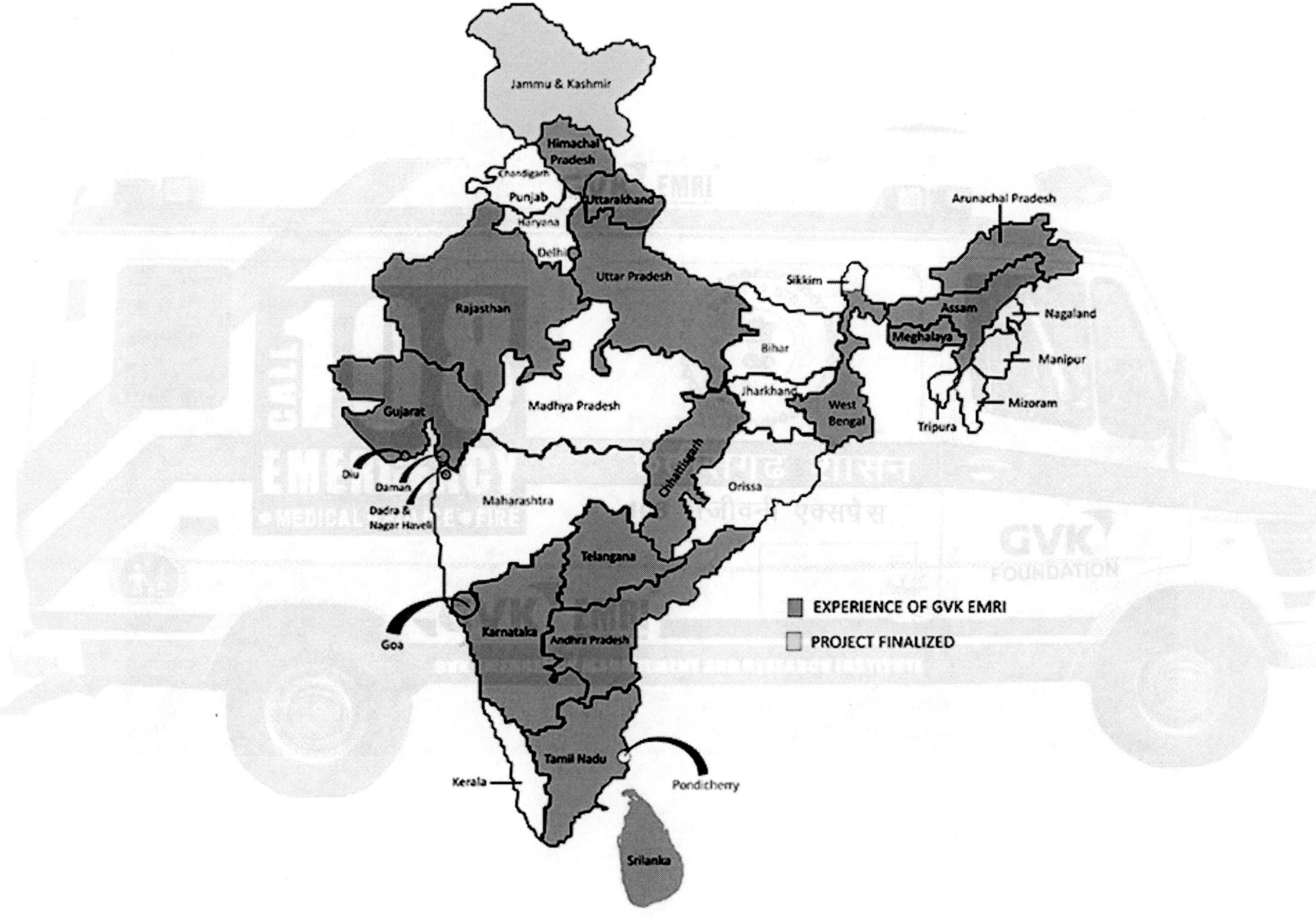
Jammu & Kashmir
Himachal Pradesh
Chandigarh
Punjab
Uttarakhand
Haryana
Delhi
Rajasthan
Uttar Pradesh
Arunachal Pradesh
Sikkim
Assam
Nagaland
Meghalaya
Bihar
Manipur
Gujarat
Madhya Pradesh
Jharkhand
West Bengal
Mizoram
Tripura
Diu
Daman
Dadra & Nagar Haveli
Chhattisgarh
Orissa
Maharashtra
Telangana
Goa
Karnataka
Andhra Pradesh
Tamil Nadu
Kerala
Pondicherry
Srilanka
EXPERIENCE OF GVK EMRI
PROJECT FINALIZED

24 X 7 અભયમ્
મહિલા હેલ્પલાઈન
સલાહ • બચાવ–મદદ
• સૂચન–માર્ગદર્શન
CALL 181 ABHAYAM
24 X 7 WOMEN HELPLINE
ADVICE • RESCUE • COUNSELING

ABSTRACT

The women helpline agencies give a speedy relief to women in distress. It can be a woman who is suffering from violence, or she needs an emergency medical treatment, counselling or any legal aid. 181 is a very important and a required agency in India as it brings help to the women at their doorstep in the shortest time possible. The women employees who provide help to the victims also undergo traumatic stress in their day-to-day work life. To study the same, sample of 150 women, both call receivers and outreach counsellors were collected. The stress level of the emergency women workers was assessed by the Organisational Role Stress (ORS) scale and the Big Five Locator test was used to study the personality type of the employees. Through this paper an attempt has been made to assess the impact of stress that the women workers working at 181 Abhayam are facing in the state of Gujarat. The results of this study revealed that the conscientiousness dimension of the personality was dependent on most of the factors causing stress. Also, most of the stress experienced by the women employees was due to the inter role distance and the role overload stress factors present in the organisation.

Key Words: *Women Helpline Agencies, Workers, and Problems Faced.*

1

INTRODUCTION

GVK EMRI in association with Government of Gujarat and Government of Uttar Pradesh was established to operate 181 Women Helpline Services. This 24×7 helpline known as Abhayam in the state of Gujarat is supported by rescue vans with counsellors and lady constable. Till date it has responded to 1.75 lakh calls out of which more than 1.0 lakh beneficiaries have received counselling.

This Scheme of Universalisation of Women Helpline is intended to provide 24 hours immediate and emergency response to women affected by violence through referral (linking with appropriate authority such as police, One Stop Centre, hospital) and information about women related government schemes programmes across the country through a single uniform number. Women Helpline (WHL) is integrated with One Stop Centre Scheme (OSC) under which one OSC has been established in every State/UT to provide integrated support and assistance to women affected by violence, both in private and public spaces under one roof. Women affected by violence and in need of redressal services are referred to OSC through WHL. Under the WHL Scheme, the States/UTs have utilised or augmented the existing women helplines through a dedicated single national number. Department of Telecommunication, Government of India has allocated short code 181 to all States/UTs which is being used by some States/UTs such as Gujarat, Delhi, Chandigarh, and Chhattisgarh as Women Helpline. Under this Scheme, States/UTs have adopted this short code 181 as Women Helpline (WHL). It is envisaged that this number is compatible with all the existing telecommunication channels whether providing post/pre-paid mobile or landline services through any public or private network i.e. GSM, CDMA, 3G and 4G etcetera. All the state/district /city level helplines whether private or public are integrated with this women helpline at the national level.

2

OBJECTIVES OF THE SCHEME AND THE TARGET GROUP

- To provide toll-free 24-hours telecom service to women affected by violence seeking support and information.
- To facilitate crisis and non-crisis intervention through referral to the appropriate agencies such as police/Hospitals/Ambulance services/District Legal Service Authority (DLSA)/Protection Officer (PO)/OSC.
- To provide information about the appropriate support services, government schemes and programmes available to the woman affected by violence, in her particular situation within the local area in which she resides or is employed.
- Information about women related programmes or schemes.

Target Group: Any woman or girl facing violence within public or private sphere of life or seeking.

The WHL is universalised through short code 181 number by augmenting/using the infrastructure of existing helplines working at the State/UT level. States/UTs have the option of locating the Helpline Centre in capital or in any other city as per their requirement. However, while selecting the location of the WHL due care needs to be taken by the States/UTs for its integration with the OSC. Similar system is in progress and has been initiated by Gujarat too.

3

GUJARAT'S INITIATIVES

"ABHYAM-181" –WOMEN HELPLINE, the state of Gujarat has always been a leader in all aspects of innovation and initiation of public services. One of the excellent example of effective public services is "108" Emergency Response Service which has touched life of citizen of Gujarat.

Government of Gujarat is taking a unique initiative in form of "181–Abhayam" Women Helpline for all women citizen of Gujarat. This will be in synchronisation and complementary system with existing "1091–Gujarat Police Helpline" and other women orientated services. For women empowerment and to support women in distress Government of Gujarat has launched 24×7 free women helpline, "181-Abhayam". "181" is a toll free number and accessible through any mobile or landline. This service has been working through the coordination of Women and Child Development Department, Home Department and GVK EMRI. Women Helpline Service established by leveraging existing resources of 108 Emergency Management Services under PPP framework between Government of Gujarat (Women and Child Development Department, Home Department) and GVK EMRI.

Initially 181 Abhayam Helpline has been functional in Ahmedabad and Surat Cities and Gandhinagar Districts. It provides information, Guidance and support to women in distress. Looking at its effectiveness the State Government has decided to expand the reach of the services in the entire State. The state wide services launched by Hon'ble Chief Minister of Gujarat, Smt. Anandiben Patel on 8th March 2015 on the occasion of International Women's Day at Gandhinagar with fleet of 45 spread across the State.

OBJECTIVES OF ABHYAM-181 WOMEN HELPLINE

- To provide 24×7 free counselling, guidance and information through centralised response centre.
- To rescue in emergent situations like domestic or any type of violence to shift women to safe places.
- Response to 100 per cent calls through technology integration.

SERVICES TO WOMEN WILL BE PROVIDED THROUGH

- Counselling, guidance and information through centralised response centre.
- Rescue in domestic or any type of violence to shift women to safe places.
- Important information will be provided like local government services, women police stations, and free legal services, counselling centre, NGOs and rescue officer.
- If any women will feel threatened or facing any violence she will be transferred to the nearest safe place for which she can call any time.

4

181 WOMEN HELPLINE SERVICES

TYPES OF SERVICES

1. Violence Against Women (VAW) Prevention

As soon as an aggrieved woman (AG) or somebody on her behalf contacts WHL, her information is attended by the call responder appointed there. Based on the urgency and the requirements explained by the caller, the responder refers her to relevant support services like medical aid, police assistance or connect her to OSC for professional counselling, shelter, legal aid etc.; if the woman needs to be rescued from a violent situation or is in urgent need of medical assistance then the PCR Van from the nearest police station or ambulance from nearest hospital/108 service would be dispatched.

2. Information of Women Empowerment Schemes and Programmes

WHL provides information about the laws, existing schemes and government programmes related to women empowerment and protection. Any woman in need of such information or someone on her behalf may call WHL which will provide this information or refer the woman to the relevant department to access the same. WHL also provides guidance to women about processes to be adopted for accessing benefits of these schemes and programmes.

3. Types of Calls received by 181

Sr. No.	*Type of Calls*	*No. of calls*	*Per cent calls received*
1.	Domestic Violence	80,940	26.40
2.	Neighbourhood Issue	16,740	13.40
3.	Physical Assault	12,350	5.40
4.	Addictions- Alcohol/Drugs/Others	14,940	7.20
5.	Other Information	9,543	1.80
6.	Stalking - Telephonic	4,578	0.50
7.	Legal issues	8,433	2.40
8.	Stress issues	6,109	1.90
9.	Other relationship issues	7,449	1.40
10.	Helpline Information	5,603	0.90
11.	Extramarital issue	5,103	1.90
12.	Enquiry Call	4,569	1.00
13.	Stalking - Physical	5,241	1.80
14.	Homelessness	5,002	2.30
15.	Custody Issue	2,719	0.90
16.	Property Issues	5,835	0.60
17.	Escalation	2,289	0.50
18.	Forced removal from residence	1,717	0.50
19.	Death Threat	1,264	0.20
20.	Rest of other call Type	1,08,510	29
	Grand Total	**3,08,934**	**100**

Fig: Types of calls received by the 181 centre.

5

SERVICE DELIVERY FRAMEWORK

ROLES AND RESPONSIBILITIES OF 181 EMPLOYEES

1. PROJECT MANAGER

2. PROJECT COORDINATOR

- The Project Coordinator is in charge for the overall smooth functioning of WHL.
- They ensure prompt and meaningful response towards every call received at the Helpline.
- They directly intervene in heinous cases in collaboration with state agencies.
- They are responsible to monitor and intervene (if required) in any ongoing calls.
- They supervise each case, takes it to a logical conclusion and later follows up with the aggrieved woman.
- They ensure effective convergence with concerned agencies/institutions.
- They facilitate redressal of issues related to non-responsiveness of State agencies/institutions in collaboration with Director, WCD.

- They are responsible for making schedules for the team and managing the team in such a way that the Helpline is up and active 24 hours a day seven days a week.
- They are responsible for taking daily, weekly and monthly reports from the Floor Supervisors and preparing periodical reports.
- They are responsible for formulating Resource Directory containing information about the relevant State and private authorities/ institutions/individuals related to women empowerment and protection.
- They are responsible for conducting advocacy meetings to create good working culture between WHL and different service providers.
- They conduct awareness generation activities within community to raise awareness around WHL.
- They monitor the functioning of WHL, conducts the performance appraisal of the staff, and facilitates capacity building, guidance and support for the team.
- They are responsible for day-to-day management of WHL team and reporting to Director, WCD and any other competent authority as and when required.

3. TEAM LEADER

- They ensure that all calls are being attended promptly and every call has been taken to its logical conclusion by the responder, as early as possible.
- They conduct regular follow up of the cases and talks with concerned authorities and departments as per the requirement of the case.
- They provide guidance to team members, manages the team and makes daily reports to the Helpline Manager for further follow up.
- They support the Helpline Manager in capacity building of the team.
- They note down the shortcomings in call handling, if any, and directs the concerned responder for further corrective action with necessary guidance.
- They will brief/de-briefs all responders before start of the duty shift and at the time of closing of the duty shift.
- They recommend closure of any case.
- They check all the closed calls and ensures that proper/needful action has been taken on each call.

- They confirm that the assistance/police help has reached/provided to the caller and also note down his/her comments/response.
- They check the missed calls and initiate response towards the same.
- They bring into the notice of Project Manager the caller/AG's dissatisfaction with the assistance provided or in case failure in providing assistance to the caller/AG is noticed.
- She advises women referred by call responders.
- She supports the Supervisor in weekly follow up with the aggrieved woman asking about the quality of service provided.
- She supports the Supervisor in gathering weekly update on any ongoing case being under police investigation or under trial.
- She supports the Supervisor in report writing process.
- In case of any contingencies and absence of Supervisor, she manages the floor.

4. TELEPHONIC COUNSELLOR

- They attend the calls; does primary referrals, does data entry and forward serious cases to Supervisor and cases which need first point counselling to Senior Call Responder.
- They provide information about the Government Schemes and programmes related to women empowerment.
- They provide all the assistance to women applying for any such above mentioned scheme or programme and guides them through the process to be adopted for accessing the same.
- They help the Supervisor in attending missed calls.
- They are responsible for other work assigned by the Response Centre.

5. SUPPORT STAFF MEMBERS

IT STAFF

- The IT staff looks after the technological aspect of WHL and ensures that it remains functional at all times.
- They follow strict proceedings to maintain privacy with regard to data generated and ensures that name and other details of aggrieved woman remain confidential in each step of case history documentation.

- They draft the daily/monthly/quarterly reports based on the MIS, web based data collection which is approved by the Helpline Manager for submission.
- With the help of Helpline Manager formulates the resource directory containing information about the relevant State and private authorities/institutions/individual related to women empowerment and protection.

MULTI-PURPOSE HELPER

- They are responsible for maintaining hygiene and sanitation at Helpline.
- They are responsible for the house keeping at WHL.

SECURITY GUARD

- They are responsible for the overall security of Helpline Centre.
- They are responsible for safety of all capital assets, furniture and equipment at WHL.

6

MODALITIES OF THE SCHEME

ACCESSING WOMEN HELPLINE

The Women Helpline is accessible 24 hours a day 7 days a week to any woman or girl suffering violence or in distress in the following manner:

- Telephone-Landlines, mobile phones through calls, SMS/text messaging, mobile apps and fax messages;
- Internet-Emails, web-posts, web-interface, social networking sites i.e. web page, Facebook, twitter, my gov, etc.

SERVICES FOR DIFFERENTLY ABLED PEOPLE

WHL is sensitive to the needs of persons who are hearing and speech impaired or people with disability. It has provision to locate/trace the number from which a call has been received. In case woman has been interrupted during her call or is unable to specify her problem or her address due to being sick/disabled then the same would be traced and within minutes WHL will facilitate an emergency response through nearest police station/hospital or OSC.

7

MANAGEMENT INFORMATION SYSTEM PROCESS

A web enabled Management Information System (MIS) has been developed to provide a user friendly and easily accessible one single portal giving due regard to the confidentiality of women affected by violence. When an aggrieved woman approaches the WHL her personal and case details will be fed into this system as per the prescribed format and a Unique ID Number would be generated through which the case would be followed by the authorities from district to central level.

This system is also used to access accurate information about the network of institutions and resources available and able to provide medical, legal, shelter support to women in any given State/UT. For the purpose, a Resource Directory is collated from resource mapping at the State level and uploaded in the computer managed by the IT Staff.

Furthermore, this software is utilised to provide information about all the schemes and programmes run by Central/State Government/UT Administration for the empowerment of women and girls. In case, a woman places a call to inquire about the same, she is provided with requisite information and guided through the process required for accessing these schemes and programmes. For example, if a woman calls WHL seeking information about widow pension scheme, the same is provided to her along with the details of officer concerned (in particular district where she resides) whom she needs to approach for accessing the same.

One Stop Centre Scheme, a web based software is adopted by the States/UTs as mentioned earlier, customised as per the WHL implementation guidelines and contextualised as per their local requirements (regional language version of the software).

8

AWARENESS GENERATION AND OUTREACH ACTIVITIES

WHL undertakes outreach and awareness generation activities to inform and encourage women to utilise its service in case of need. For women to contact WHL, they first need to know about the service and understand what it can do for them. Hence, outreach and awareness-generation activities are therefore key components of a WHL.

Outreach and awareness-generation activities take the WHL service to women and ensures accessibility of the Helpline to the most marginalised women of the State. In addition, these activities also act as a deterrent measure by ensuring the prevention of VAW through creation of a society which denounces violence upon women. For the purpose, IEC activities at State/UT level are organised for spreading awareness about the Scheme and sensitising all concerned.

The institutional mechanism under MWCD and other concerned departments at the State/district/village/urban/rural level i.e. PO, ASHA, ANM, AWW, PRIs along with civil society groups, self-help groups (SHG), individuals are utilised for creating awareness.

Different awareness-generation strategies including mass publicity campaign through distribution of leaflets, pamphlets, brochures, posters and dissemination of information through public transport system i.e. buses, auto-rickshaw, taxis, media channels (newspapers, radio and television), public conferences, special events such Women's Day, interface with youth through school and college based outreach and more are utilised for the same purpose.

Thus, after 108, the state government and GVK EMRI have launched 181 - the Abhyam Women Helpline for all women in Gujarat. The helpline, launched in collaboration with the home and women and child welfare departments, is synchronised with the existing “1091-Gujarat Police Helpline” and other women-oriented services.

The free 24x7 helpline, 181, is a toll-free number to support women in distress and is accessible through any mobile or landline. Any woman can access the 181 Abhyam helpline for counselling, guidance, information and also for rescue from various threatening situations including domestic violence. The helpline aims to provide 24×7 free counselling, guidance and information through a centralised response centre. The helpline also aims to effect rescues in situations like domestic or other violence to and shift vulnerable women to safe places.

“Services provided through 181 will include rescue from domestic violence to shift women to safe places, important information is provided on local government services, women’s police stations, free legal services and counselling centres, NGOs and rescue officers. If a women is threatened or facing violence she is transferred to the nearest safe place from where she is able to call at any time.”

Also, teenagers older than 14 years, and all women in general can call the helpline. Information given at the time of call is kept confidential. Women facing violence be it physical, sexual, mental, financial, at work place and those facing problems in marital relationships are helped. Matters related to child birth, legal first-hand information, as well as matters related to finances and professions are also discussed under 181 Women Helpline Services.

SPECIAL IEC CAMPAIGN THROUGH STREET PLAY

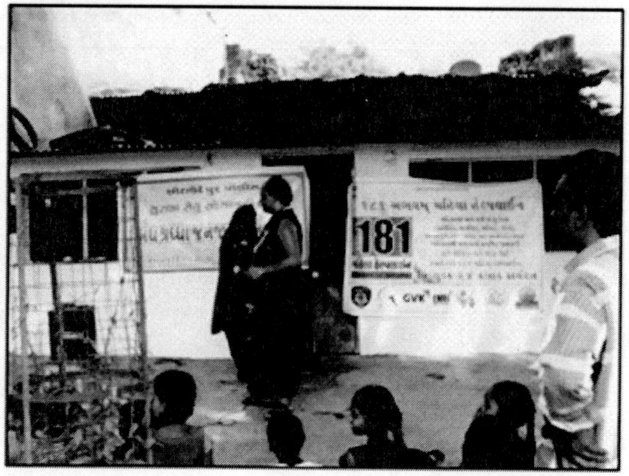

181- COMMUNITY AWARENESS CAMPAIGN (ASHA WORKERS)

181- COMMUNITY AWARENESS CAMPAIGN (VILLAGE DEMO)

181- COMMUNITY AWARENESS CAMPAIGN (SCHOOLS)

REFRESHERS TRAINING OF OSCC AND 181 COUNSELLORS

9

RATIONALE OF THE RESEARCH

There are various researches done on the victims of problems like domestic violence, harassment, or any sort of violence against women; but there are very few researches done on the workers who are behind the process of rescuing these very victims and helping them be safe and secured. Therefore, the main motive of taking this research was to identify the level of stress that is faced by the women working in 181 helpline agency.

OBJECTIVE OF THE RESEARCH

1. To assess the stress levels of working women in the 181 helpline emergency toll free number national service.
2. To study the association between the personality and stress levels of the employees.
3. To provide the women employees with the coping techniques to overcome the impact of stress.

10

LITERATURE REVIEW

STRESS

In psychology, stress is a feeling of strain and pressure. It is good to have small amount of stress as it helps in improvement of athletic performance more popularly known as positive stress. It is due to mild or moderate stress which is not harmful for the body. Positive stress helps in motivation and adaptation to the competitive environment, it also helps in learning, improving creativity and increasing one's efficiency at work finally leading to higher level of self-esteem. But, there is also a downside to excessive stress, it can lead to heart strokes, ulcers, mental illness like depression thus leading to extreme harm to the body.

CAUSES OF STRESS

Stress can be both internal and external, the internal part deals with the creation of internal perceptions that can cause an individual to experience negative emotions such as anxiety or any other type of emotions that get developed by the environment, like pressure, discomfort, etc., which can cause immense distress. The external stress is usually related to environment. It depends on people to people and the causes can be diverse and individualised.There can be many forms of stress, the stress in workplace can be due to hectic schedule, heavy load of work, less time for family and problems in relationships, also financial problems and likewise.

STRESS IN WORKPLACE

The pressures that workers face are new bosses, computer surveillance of production, fewer health and retirement benefits, and the feeling they have to work longer and harder just to maintain their current economic status. Workers at every level are experiencing increased tension and uncertainty.

Work setting creates physical stress because of noise, lack of privacy, poor lighting, poor ventilation, poor temperature control or inadequate sanitary facilities.

Criminal justice personnel, firefighters, ambulance drivers, helpline agency workers, military personnel and disaster teams witness many terrible scenes and are exposed to personal danger routinely. Occasionally a particularly bad episode will stay with them, appearing in memory flashbacks and nightmares. Sleep disturbance, guilt, fearfulness and physical complaints may follow. Even ordinary jobs can become traumatic: e.g. a co-worker, boss or client physically threatens an employee. Such events can create post-traumatic stress disorder (PTSD).

"Workplace stress" is defined as the harmful physical and emotional responses that can happen when there is a conflict between job demands on the employee and the amount of control an employee has over meeting these demands. In general, the combination of high demands in a job and a low amount of control over the situation can lead to stress.

The article mentions about the stress that is caused due to the hard supervision of the manager. According to the article, stress has been defined as the relationship between a person and his/her environment that is perceived to be unbalanced in terms of one's physical and psychological resources and the demands of the situation (Lazarus and Folkman, 1984).

Workplace stress is often related to the design of the job, the culture and environment of the workplace setting, relationships that exist in the workplace, or some combination of these (Yoo *et al.*, 2009). It also mentions that due to the long working hours it gets difficult for the supervisors to detach themselves form their job and so it has a negative effect on their mood and behaviour. It is difficult to tell the difference between the symptoms of stress and the stressor; therefore, the article has focused on viewing the overall perception of stress of the supervisor. In many of their studies the researchers have placed their supervisor's aggression as displaced aggression. Displaced aggression is the "redirection of a [person's] harm doing behaviour from a primary to a secondary target or victim" (Tedeschi and Norman, 1985, p. 30). Therefore, when there is a problem in decision-making from the authority and increased workload the supervisor will not turn towards the authority instead according to the research, will take out their anger on the less powerful subordinate.

After a few data collections and research material the article concludes that the supervisor can loosen the end of frustration between them and the subordinates by engaging in healthy buffering mechanisms of a moderate level of physical exercise. Thus, the more they try to balance their work life and personal life they will be less aggressive and will be able to balance their stress in a better way.

Kulkarni, P. and Deoras, N. (2017) in their article talked about the various factors that contribute in the workplace stress in India. The workload is not the only reason that an individual faces stress, there are other reasons such as poor coordination in the team, conflicting job expectations, low pay and more. "It is important to look beyond the workload. How talent is managed and communication is done play a key role. For example, the way managers speak to subordinates can impact their morale," says Anuradha Sriram, Director, Benefits, Towers Watson India.

The culture and the environment can lead to suffocation at work. The strict rules and regulations along with dissatisfying rewards also hamper the performance of the employee or any other worker. The article concludes by talking about how friends and family play the most important part in coping up with stress and how they can help an individual in making better decisions by giving him/her the support required.

Occupational stress is stress related to one's job. Occupational stress often stems from unexpected responsibilities and pressures that do not align with a person's knowledge, skills, or expectations, inhibiting one's ability to cope. Occupational stress can increase when workers do not feel supported by supervisors or colleagues, or feel as if they have little control over work processes.

Spector, P. (2002) in this article talks about the occupational stress faced by the employees. The stress can take different forms of problems with time, i.e. if the stress is for a short period of time it will lead to anxiety. The physical health problem to be seen in short-term stress is headache and stomach distress, and in the long-term process is seen as cardiovascular disease.

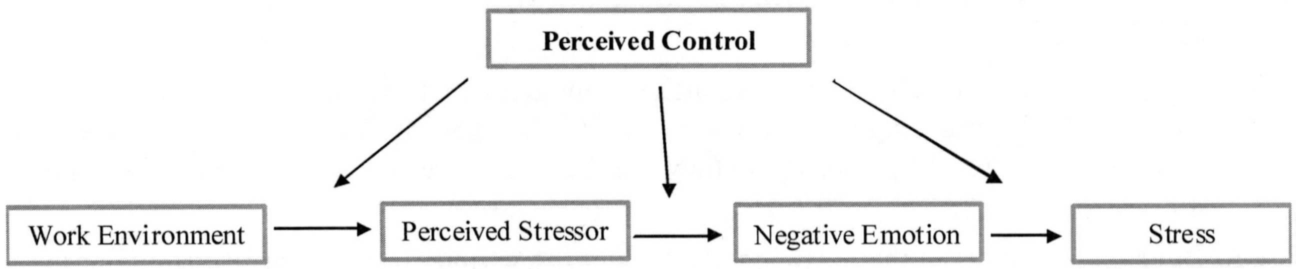

Fig: Control Model of Occupation Stress.

The theory of this article is based on a Control - Stress Model. The process begins with the workplace environment. All of the day the employees experience and perceive all sorts of conditions and events. Some of which are not so important but some of them are big events which can be perceived as threatening to the physical and psychological well-being of the employee. These stressors can lead to negative emotions or reactions, which can be anger and anxiety to name a few. Thus, these behavioural and physical stressors can lead to stress. The most important element in this model is the perceived control, as it plays a role in all the steps till the result is concluded as stress.

THE STRAINS FACED IN OCCUPATIONAL STRESS CAN BE OF TWO TYPES

Behavioural Strains- It includes the actions that are taken by the individuals to cope up with their stress. They can be positive actions like finding ways to solve problems by talking, changing patterns. They can be negative actions such as smoking, taking alcohol, not coming to work at all, or fighting in the workplace in order to cope up with stress.

Physical Strains- These strains are related to the burn out that takes place after doing a lot of hard work and also the negative emotions that are faced physiologically. All these strains can cause problems like increased blood pressure, elevated heart rate, or even release of hormones that are associated with stress.

The conclusion of this article is with the fact that control plays a big role in coping up with stress. The individuals who have high control will not perceive most of the events taking place in the workplace as stressors as compared to the individuals who have less control.

The occupational stress as a subject has been recognised in United States and many other industrialised countries as a major health issue. It is important to maintain the health and well-being of the employees in the company; therefore, the companies have to pay much more attention in taking decisions which are in favour of the better health and well-being of the employees of the company.

In the article the author gives several definitions of stress out of which one is: Hans Selye, one of the most influential writers on the subject has described it in his monumental Stress in Health and Disease (1) as: '... associated with a great variety of essentially dissimilar problems, such as surgical trauma, burns, emotional arousal, mental or physical effort, fatigue, pain, fear, the need for concentration, the humiliation of frustration, the loss of blood, intoxication with drugs or environmental pollutants, or even with the kind of unexpected success that requires an individual to reformulate his lifestyle. Stress is present in the businessman under constant pressure; in the athlete straining to win a race; in the air traffic controller who bears continuous responsibility for hundreds of lives; in the husband helplessly watching his wife's slow, painful death from cancer; in a race horse, its jockey and the spectator who bets on them'.

Further in the article it talk about how the definition of stress changes in each and every situation and is widely being misused by the modern world. The concept of stress came into picture by studying the correlation between the inside and the outside event that are faced by an individual.

Stress by this article is described in three ways:

STRESS AS STIMULUS- It plays a part in the activity of stress but it cannot be defined solely in terms of the stimulus. It can be in different ways and can have different responses. If a stimulus is brought a number of times the response will slowly start to wash away and the individual will get 'adapted' to that stimulus of stress resulting in no response.

STRESS AS RESPONSE- The most influential theorist of stress seems to have been Hans Selye whose definition was: 'Stress is the nonspecific response of the body to any demand' (1). Selye claims that the non-specific response is composed of the General Adaptation Syndrome (GAS) which results from the prolonged action of 'diverse noxious agents' (so that the nature of the stimulus does, after all, play a part). In his original experiments he apparently noted the similar features of patients suffering from a variety of different severe diseases; in particular a triad of adrenal (cortex) enlargement, thymus gland involution and gastric/duodenal ulceration. Some years later the same triad was observed in rats injected with crude extracts of hormone derived from cattle. The syndrome could also be induced by other 'toxic' extracts.

STRESS AS A STIMULUS AS WELL AS A RESPONSE- The definition of stress can be more properly told by combining the two i.e. stimulus and response with stress. In simple words stress is the response to a subjectively felt stressful stimulus. Thus, if there was no response then it clearly brings out that there was no stressful stimulus, stating the fact that this explanation of stress is best suited amongst the other two given above.

The article concluded that stress is not appropriately used and so it should be used less and in a proper manner. It is a synonym to ignorance and that's the main reason that it should not be used in clinical practices. Instead the words pressure and tension should be taken in practice.

PERSONALITY AND STRESS

Snigdha Rai and V.V. Ajith Kumar (2012) the main objective of this study is to investigate the relationship between five factor personality model and role stress. Stress in the workplace is increasingly a critical problem for employees, employers and for the organisation as a whole, but it is inevitable and a necessary part of life (Doublet, 2000). Empirical researches in this area have demonstrated the direct and indirect costs of stress on individual employee's performance and performance of organisation as a whole (Ortqvist and Wincent, 2006). Studies also indicate that the amount of experienced role stress is partly depended on the personality predispositions of the employee concerned (Keenan and McBain, 1979).

Within an organisational context, the term 'role' can be defined as a set of expectations applied to the incumbent of a particular position by the incumbent and by role senders within and beyond an organisational boundary (Banton, 1965). 5). Role stress originate when an individual in a particular work role is torn by conflicting job demands or doing things he/she does not think are part of the job specifications (Cooper and Marshall, 1976). It is also mentioned that personality plays a role in the way a person experiences and copes with stress. It is generally believed that the competitive, aggressive, and anxious people are more prone towards experiencing stress (Ivancevich *et al.,* 1982, Cooper, Dewe and O'Driscol).

Studies in India have also attempted Researchers offer a range of frame to establish the degree of association or works relating personality and the causal relationships of stress with other variables such as organisational, job, leadership, communicational and personal factors (Pestonjee, 1992). In many studies it has also been shown that the Five Factor Model (FFM) of personality are meaningful drivers of individual behaviour and performance (James and Mazerolle, 2002; Zhao and Seibert, 2006). O'Brien and Delongis (1996) used the five factor model of personality and dimensions of the social context to understand how people cope with stress.

The result ultimately suggested that, each of the five personality dimensions examined in their study were independently and significantly related to role stress and its dimensions.

Shimon L. Dolan, Marie R. van Ameringen and André Arsenault (1992). This study examines social support as a correlate of perceived job demands and psychological strain and as a moderator of the relationship between stimulus and response, according to personality traits. Separate analysis on each personality type reflect this general trend with the notable exception of the COOL CAT type who seems to exhibit only anxiety as a significant correlate of extrinsic demands. To conclude there was some support given to the role of social support as a moderator variable in the relationships between occupational demands and psychological strains. Such an effect seems to interact with both personality traits and type of job demands. In more specific terms, certain personality types may not even seek social support when experiencing either intrinsic or extrinsic demands. Or the lack of social support might reinforce certain personal attitudes with increasing demands.

Robert E. Gilbert (1985) developed his study in the context to understand how personality and stress are dependent in case of presidency. In his study it was mentioned that those who reach the office of President find themselves subjected to a constant stream of stressful situations which may well compound their susceptibility to cardiovascular disease and which may also increase the likelihood of their contracting various non-cardiovascular illnesses. Woodrow Wilson once remarked, "I work hard, of course…but it is not that that tells on a fellow. It's the anxiety attending the handling of…affairs in which you seem to be touching quicksilver."

There are medical indications that cardiovascular disease occurs more frequently in persons of a certain personality type and that stress, and the failure to cope with stress, are contributing factors. Recent research findings raise the possibility that tension may well reduce immunity to most, if not to all, diseases and that it likely is linked to any number of life-threatening illnesses. To conclude he also mentions that the personality traits which draw individuals to the Presidency and the great stress they encounter there are vital factors in any study of presidential pathology. Inability to cope with the stresses of power and responsibility is an additional factor worthy of note. Thus, personality plays a vital role in the job of a president and how they manage their stress and cope with it also depends on their personality.

B. Lucile Bowie (1966) in her review of the book 'Constructive Behaviour: Stress, Personality, and Mental Health by E. Paul Torrance', talks about the thesis of the book which says that "mental functioning and stress are key factors" in the development of a healthy personality. The main emphasis in this book is given to the concept of healthy personality development and mental functioning as responding constructively to stress and not merely accepting or adapting to stress. The book that has been reviewed has been divided in four parts out of which part four of the book, which makes up for half of the book deals with mental functioning. Using J. P. Guilford's Model of the Structure of the Intellect as a theoretical base, the author describes, elaborates and illustrates the role of each mental operation (cognition, memory, convergent production, divergent production, and evaluation) in coping with stress. By stating that "if an individual's mental abilities and operations are functioning, he will be able to cope constructively with stress." The practical procedures recommended in this section of the book are keys to releasing the creative thought processes of the mind which could revolutionise the educative process and lead to maximum development of students' potentialities. A unique feature of the book is the manner in which the author actively engages the reader in utilising the problem-solving approach. The reader is urged to present his solution to a problem which can be evaluated against research findings and solutions proposed by the author. The author in conclusion also offered teachers of elementary schools many practical suggestions for applying this knowledge and assisting students to develop more productive and constructive modes of coping with the everyday stressors of life that they come across.

COPING WITH STRESS

Gustems-Carnicer, J. and Calderón, C. (2013) in this study it is mentioned that coping techniques can play a very important role in dealing with stress in a workplace. The most accepted definition of coping strategy is by Lazarus and Folkman (1986), who define it as an adaptive response to a specific stressor. This is the process through a person seeks to deals with stress, using a wide range of psychological strategies and mechanisms (both cognitive and behavioural) in order to reduce, minimise, control or tolerate it (Parker and Endler, 1992). A stressful situation is one that is experienced by an individual as threatening and harmful, and it may alter or interfere with his or her physical and/or psychological well-being (Vaughn and Roesch, 2003).

Authors like Lazarus and Folkman (1986) state that coping has two functions: one is targeted at the objective problem, at the demand or task, and aims to solve the problem, while the other targets the individual's emotions in order to modify his or her experience of the situation, and to reduce the tension, physiological activity and emotional reaction.

Sidle, S. (2008) in this article talks about how the manager has to select from many options, any one option that helps the employees reduce their stress in workplace. It is also mentioned how, Katherine Richardson and Hannah Rothstein of Baruch

College in their recent study compare the outcomes of a variety of workplace stress management interventions. They classified interventions as primary, secondary and tertiary. The section that deals with the primary intervention states that there should be alteration done in the source of stress by redesigning jobs to give employees greater flexibility and more decision-making control.

The secondary management intervention deals with including courses that teach meditation and or time management. The last, i.e. the tertiary section deals with helping the employees to recover from their stress by giving them access to counselling in the Employee Assistance Plan (EPA) to help them talk and overcome the challenging situations that they have been facing.

In conclusion, Richardson and Rothstein in their meta-analysis, could help a lot of individuals more through the secondary intervention technique. They also later sub-divided their study and placed secondary intervention under the name of cognitive-behavioural approach. The second term given to secondary intervention was Relaxation approach as it included meditation. The primary intervention was named as Organisational approach as it deals with making changes in the designing of the working of the organisation.

The best technique that was chosen as the most widely used was the cognitive-behavioural approach in which the employees can be taught techniques for how to cope up with stress in their workplace.

Topper, E. (2003) in this article mentioned different ways of dealing with stress is mentioned which are:-

Using our Special Skills-it talks about how we should use and show our skills as it will help us be satisfied in the type of job we are working in. Job satisfaction is the biggest solution to lesser stress as there is no frustration of working under any pressure or working for a job you don't like.

Learning the fact which is, we should be good to ourselves- we should try to take out some time from our busy schedules and take a walk, eat outside, anything to get some personal tie away from the desk.

Accepting the fact-we should try to accept the fact that we cannot control or manage everything. Thus, we should take the criticism as a form of constructive feedback which will help to improve our quality of work.

Work out-we should not forget to work out as the exercise helps our body to release endorphins which help the body to cope during stress.

Therefore, these were the few techniques that help us cope up with stress in an easier and healthy manner.

Janina C. Latack' and Stephen J. Havlovic (1992) in their article talked about the coping mechanisms for stress in workplace. The few methods used and other researches performed to form new methods of coping.

Researchers have defined the concept of 'stressful', specifying the dimensions of a situation that will call forth coping responses. For example, Coyne, Aldwin and Lazarus (1981) state that 'coping refers to efforts, both cognitive and behavioural, to manage environmental and internal demands and conflicts affecting an individual that tax or exceed a person's resources'. Dewe (1987) refers to 'active or passive attempts to respond to a situation of threat with the aim of removing the threat or reducing the discomfort.'

From the many definitions given in the article a few are:

1. **Folkman and Lazarus (1980) -** 'Coping is defined as the cognitive and behavioural efforts made to master, tolerate, or reduce external and internal demands and conflicts among them'.
2. **Kinicki and Latack (1990) -** 'Coping is conceptualised as cognitive and behavioural efforts to manage the internal and external demands of person-environment transactions appraised as stressful (Folkman and Lazarus, 1985; Folkman et al., 1986)'
3. **O'Neill and Zeichner (1985) -** 'Coping with stress has been defined as the cognitive and behavioural efforts that master, minimize, tolerate, or reduce internal and environmental demands' (Lazarus, 1980). Two major classes of coping responses have been formulated (Billings and Moos, 1982; Folkman and Lazarus, 1980; Pearlin and Schooler, 1978): (a) problem-focused coping which regulates stressful person-environment interactions, and (b) emotion-focused coping which regulates stressful emotions.
4. **Zappert and Weinstein (1985) -** 'the coping style index included items related to the ability to set limits and pace oneself, confidence in one's judgment, seeking feedback or information when faced with a problem, and attempting to be the best at all one does; ... the coping strain index included items related to difficulties controlling temper or emotions, impatience, heightened sensitivity to criticism, self-doubt and self-blame, and inaction when confronting problems;.."
5. **Parasuraman and Cleek (1984) -** 'coping behaviours were defined conceptually as individuals' overt attempts to alleviate or respond to stressful conditions at work.'

To elaborate the concept of coping methods in terms of the definition, the article has mentioned something called comprehensiveness.

COMPREHENSIVENESS- It includes two coping dimensions: 'Focus of coping' it is the main problem or the individual's emotional reaction to stress. 'Method of coping' they are the different ways that are used by the individual to cope with the problem of stress. It can be behavioural vs cognitive, social vs solitary, or escape vs resignation.

In case of methods of coping the emotion-focused coping can also be behavioural in method such as exercising more or smoking (Billings and Moos, 1981). The problem-focused coping can also be cognitive such as taking extra care to plan and organize (Latack, 1986; Parasuraman and Cleek, 1984) or behavioural, such as trying to find out more about the situation (Billing and Moos, 1981).

It is also mentioned that in cases of job related coping methods the two most popular styles are used, i.e. Control and Escape. The part dealing with controlled approach is when the person will take charge and look into the problem to find solutions in order to deal with it. The other is when the person will try to escape from the problem to avoid making any scene and going away silently. Both the approaches focus on the problem from cognitive and emotional aspect.

The other method mentioned above is of social vs solitary. In social the person will seek help from others to understand the situation and take their help to gather as much information required to solve the problem and reduce stress. In the latter part the person will try to do everything on their own and not bother to talk help from anyone i.e. be unsocial and try coping alone.

The method of social coping is by the far most central method used. As the support of friends and family is given high priority to cope up with the problem of stress both mentally and physically. The article concludes by explaining some old techniques of coping and some new blue prints that can be used in the process of coping which can further help the organisations to run a better company with mentally and physically fit employees.

SETHI, A. (1982) conducted a research on, 'Stress Coping'. The research has listed some techniques through which we can cope with stress in general.

The personal coping techniques-These techniques include meditation, problem-solving, self-analysis, decision-making, gestalt's approaches, and biofeedback. These are the techniques have been taken keeping in mind the problems that occur due to stress which are, cardiovascular reactions, absenteeism, lower productivity, job dissatisfaction, staff turnover, low motivation and many more.

The organisational coping strategies-These are the strategies used in the organisation to cope up with stress in which the organisation is taking efforts to help employees deal with their problems, they include taking the risk of developing new ways of working and changing the old ways. As the article mentions power is a very important element in coping with stress, thus, the organisation should make the managers till the subordinate level aware of the power that they have and the abilities they have and that can be used in the betterment of the organisation. As powerlessness can lead to stress and frustration at a very fast speed.

Life career planning- The person should be made aware of their own capabilities through courses and their own reality before they jump into taking the big decision of choosing a career. They should be made to take self-improvement programmes and their qualities should be appreciated by the organisation and the community around them. There should be a psychological approach taken in order to cope with their organisational and personal stress by increasing authenticity, recognition of interpersonal culture, and reality orientation.

The article concludes with mentioning the importance of coping techniques because without these techniques the person will fail to realise his/her development goals as they might not have grip on their life as they are in conflict with themselves. Meditation is focused more as is said to be the most effective technique as it sharpens ones perception to look at the environment, letting go of the pressure building in the body and listening to one's body balance which will later help in gaining control of their situation. Thus, meditation will help them look at the bigger picture instead of getting in the race of competitiveness.

11

METHOD

TOOLS

The quantitative data was collected by using the Organisational Role Stress (ORS) Scale by Pareek (1983). Here, role refers to a position one occupies in a social system, and is defined by the functions one performs in response to the expectations of the significant members of the social system and one's expectation from that position or office.

Stress is built up in the concept of role. Whenever there is conflict between the self and the roles that the person occupies, there is a potential for role stress. A role stress has been defined as 'anything about an organisational role that produces adverse consequences for the individual' (Kahn and Quinn, 1970:41). The concept of role and its two related aspects, role space and role set, have a built-in potential for conflict and stress. Therefore, role is an obligational concept in which there are expectation from both the sender's side and occupant's side.

The ORS was used to measure 10 role dimensions, i.e.,

1. Inter Role Distance (IRD)
2. Role Stagnation (RS)
3. Role Expectation Conflict (REC)

4. Role Erosion (RE)
5. Role Overload (RO)
6. Role Isolation (RI)
7. Personal Inadequacy (PI)
8. Self-Role Distance (SRD)
9. Role Ambiguity (RA)
10. Resource Inadequacy (RIn)

1. **Inter Role Distance**: When an individual occupies more than one role there are bound to be conflicts between them. And with individuals occupying multiple roles in various groups etc. inter role conflicts are quite common.
2. **Role Stagnation**: When an individual has held on to a role for quite a considerable amount of time, is very comfortably settled, and after that he is asked to take on to a new role he/she may experience this stress of role stagnation when they are promoted.
3. **Role Expectation Conflict**: When there are conflicting expectations from different people e.g. Boss, subordinates, peers etc., and then the role occupant may experience this type of stress.
4. **Role Erosion**: When an organisation redefines and creates certain new roles and individual is supposed to adjust to it then he/she may have a feeling of his old role being eroded.
5. **Role Overload**: Too much of expectations from an individual by significant others in the role set leads to role overload. It is more likely to occur where role occupants lack power and there are large variations in the expected output and when delegation or assistance cannot procure more time.
6. **Role Isolation**: An individual may feel that certain roles are psychologically closer to him while others are at much distance (The criterion for which is the frequency and ease of interaction. It is basically a gap between existing and desired linkages.
7. **Personal Inadequacy**: In case a person is not competent in terms of skills required for a particular job or has had no time or training to prepare for the desired role he may experience stress and thus feel inadequate or incompetent for the job.
8. **Self-Role Distance**: When the expectations from the role and self-concept do not match then stress arises. e.g. An introvert given the job of a salesman.

9. **Role Ambiguity**: Role ambiguity is usually experienced when the roles may be newly created and are not well defined. The individual is not clear about the various expectation people have from his role. It may be due to lack of information available or lack of available cues.
10. **Resource Inadequacy**: When resources such as information, people, material, finance or facilities are not available to a role occupant resource inadequacy is experienced.

ORS is a 5 point Likert scale (0 to 4), containing five items for each role stress dimensions. Thus, the scale contains 50 items under these 10 dimensions.

The Big Five Locator Questionnaire was also used to check the personality type of the employees and interpret if the individual stress dimension was dependent or independent to the individual personality type. The test measured five factors namely,

1. Adjustment (A)
2. Sociability (S)
3. Openness to Experience (O)
4. Agreeableness (Ag)
5. Conscientiousness (C)

1. **Adjustment** (*sensitive/nervous* vs. *secure/confident*). The tendency to experience unpleasant emotions easily, such as anger, anxiety, depression, and vulnerability. Adjustment also refers to the degree of emotional stability and impulse control and is sometimes referred to by its low pole, "emotional stability". A high need for stability manifests itself as a stable and calm personality, but can be seen as uninspiring and unconcerned. A low need for stability causes a reactive and excitable personality, often very dynamic individuals, but they can be perceived as unstable or insecure.

2. **Sociability** (*outgoing/energetic* vs. *solitary/reserved*). Energy, positive emotions, surgency, assertiveness, sociability and the tendency to seek stimulation in the company of others, and talkativeness. High sociability is often perceived as attention-seeking, and domineering. Low sociability causes a reserved, reflective personality, which can be perceived as aloof or self-absorbed.

3. **Openness to experience** (*inventive/curious* vs. *consistent/cautious*). Appreciation for art, emotion, adventure, unusual ideas, curiosity, and variety of experience. Openness reflects the degree of intellectual curiosity, creativity and a preference for novelty and variety a person has. It is also described as the extent to which a person is imaginative or independent and depicts a personal preference for a variety of activities over a strict routine. High openness can be perceived as unpredictability or lack of focus, and more likely to engage in risky behaviour or drug taking. Moreover, individuals with high openness are said to pursue self-actualisation specifically by seeking out intense, euphoric experiences. Conversely, those with low openness seeks to gain fulfillment through perseverance and are characterised as pragmatic and data-driven sometimes even perceived to be dogmatic and closed-minded.

4. **Agreeableness** (*friendly/compassionate* vs. *challenging/detached*). A tendency to be compassionate and cooperative rather than suspicious and antagonistic towards others. It is also a measure of one's trusting and helpful nature, and whether a person is generally well-tempered or not. High agreeableness is often seen as naive or submissive. Low agreeableness personalities are often competitive or challenging people, which can be seen as argumentativeness or untrustworthiness.

5. **Conscientiousness** (*efficient/organised* vs. *easy-going/careless*). A tendency to be organised and dependable, show self-discipline, act dutifully, aim for achievement, and prefer planned rather than spontaneous behaviour. High conscientiousness is often perceived as stubbornness and obsession. Low conscientiousness is associated with flexibility and spontaneity, but can also appear as sloppiness and lack of reliability.

SAMPLE

In this study, sample of 150 women working at 181 Women Helpline Centre was taken. Data from 33 places at state, division, and district level namely Surat, Bharuch, Dahod, Vadodara, Valsad, Bhavnagar, Rajkot, Jamnagar, Ahmedabad, Gandhinagar etc was collected. The target respondents were the women employees of 181 Women Helpline centre of two categories, Call Receivers and Outreach Counsellors.

TESTS APPLIED

To analyse the quantitative data, statistical techniques of mean, ANOVA and chi-square were employed. ANOVA was applied to check if there is any significant difference between the stress caused and the age of the individual. ANOVA was also applied on the stress factors and the personality types. Furthermore, chi-square tests were applied to check the dependence of individual stress dimension with individual personality type.

DATA ANALYSIS

The quantitative data analysis was done using the Statistical Package for the Social Sciences (SPSS) software.

RESULTS

TEST: 1 Average Score: Stress

Stress Dimension	IRD	RS	REC	RE	RO	RI	PIn	SRD	RA	RIN
Internal Mean	7.15	5.34	5.48	7.60	4.96	6.43	5.76	4.79	4.05	4.94

Average Score was taken out to measure stress through the factors of Organisational Role Stress (ORS) scale. The highest internal mean computed is 7.60 of the Role Erosion (RE) factor. This means that the maximum stress to respondents is caused because the organisation keeps redefining and creating new roles and the employees find it difficult to adjust to it. The lowest average is 4.05 of the Role Ambiguity (RA) factor. This means that the employees are pretty clear about their roles in the organisation, also that they are well created and well designed.

Internal Mean also reveals that most of the stress is caused by the factors: Inter Role Distance (IRD) which means that the employees occupy more than one role in their organisation, Role Expectation Conflict (REC) which means that the employees have to play different roles in conflicting expectations and situations from different people, Role Isolation (RI) happens when an individual feels that certain roles are psychologically closer to her than others and Personal Inadequacy (Pl) factor. PI demonstrates that the employees aren't competent in their job and that why are stressed.

TEST: Average Score: Personality

Adjustment	*Sociability*	*Openness to Experience*	*Agreeableness*	*Conscientiousness*
48.06	48.59	44.29	53.60	57.33

Average score of the personality types of the Big Five Locator personality test was also taken out. The highest score is 57.33 of the personality type-Conscientiousness. This shows that there is a tendency to be organised and dependable in the employees of the organisation. Furthermore, it explains self-discipline, high aim for achievement, and prefer planned rather spontaneous behaviour in the women employees of the organisation. The lowest average score is 44.29 of the personality type-Openness to Experience or Change. Openness to experience is the extent to which a person is imaginative or independent and depicts a personal preference for a variety of activities over a strict routine. High openness can be perceived as unpredictability or lack of focus.

TEST: 2 ANOVA (Stress and Personality)

Analysis of Variance (ANOVA)-hypothesis-testing technique was used to test the factors of role stress scale and the personality types by examining the variances of samples that are taken for the research. ANOVA test helped determine whether the differences between the samples were simply due to random error (sampling errors) or whether there were systematic effects that caused the mean of one test factors to differ from the mean in another.

H1: There is significant difference between the stress caused and the personality type.

Ho: There is no significant difference between the stress caused and the personality type.

ANOVA[a]						
Model		*Sum of Squares*	*df*	*Mean Square*	*F*	*Sig.*
1	Regression	4.28	1	4.28	.190	.663[b]
	Residual	2855.28	127	22.48		
	Total	**2859.57**	**128**			
a. Dependent Variable: Personality						
b. Predictors: (Constant), Stress						

Regression test was done to check the hypotheses about independent categorical variables. Regression measured the difference that changes in an independent variable and further makes in a dependent variable. In the ANOVA, the categorical variable is effect coded, therefore each category's mean was compared to the grand mean. In the regression, the categorical variable is dummy coded, therefore each test's intercept was compared to the reference test's intercept.

Here the significant value is 0.66 is greater than 0.05. So null hypothesis is accepted. So, there is no significant difference being made by the dependent variable-personality in causing stress to the employees of the organisation.

Test: 3 To check whether Age affects stress or not

Analysis of Variance (ANOVA)-hypothesis-testing technique was used to test the factors of role organisational stress scale and the personality types by examining the variances of samples that are taken for the research. ANOVA test was used to check if the organisational role stress factors were affected by the age of the employees of the organisation.

When ANOVA was applied Sum of squares, Degrees of Freedom (df), Mean Square, F test was also done between groups and within groups. F variable is the ratio of two independent chi-square variables divided by their respective degrees of freedom and further significant value was obtained.

ANOVA to stress

H2: There is significant difference between the age group and stress factor Inter Role Distance.

Ho: There is no significant difference between the age group and stress factor Inter Role Distance.

ANOVA					
IRD_TOTAL_					
	Sum of Squares	*df*	*Mean Square*	*F*	*Sig.*
Between Groups	278.25	12	23.18	1.37	.18
Within Groups	1941.24	115	16.88		
Total	**2219.50**	**127**			

Interpretation: here significant value is 0.18 which is greater than 0.05. So null hypothesis is accepted which says there is no significant difference between age group and Inter Role Distance.

H3: There is significant difference between the age group and stress factor Role Stagnation.

Ho: There is no significant difference between the age group and stress factor Role Stagnation.

ANOVA					
RS TOTAL					
	Sum of Squares	***df***	***Mean Square***	***F***	***Sig.***
Between Groups	200.86	12	16.73	.96	.48
Within Groups	1986.60	115	17.27		
Total	**2187.46**	**127**			

Interpretation: here significant value is 0.48 which is greater than 0.05. So null hypothesis is accepted which says there is no significant difference between age group and Role Stagnation.

H4: There is significant difference between the age group and stress factor Role Expectation Conflict.

Ho: There is no significant difference between the age group and stress factor Role Expectation Conflict.

ANOVA					
REC TOTAL					
	Sum of Squares	***df***	***Mean Square***	***F***	***Sig.***
Between Groups	206.98	12	17.24	1.388	.18
Within Groups	1428.89	115	12.42		
Total	**1635.87**	**127**			

Interpretation: here significant value is 0.18 which is greater than 0.05. So null hypothesis is accepted which says there is no significant difference between age group and Role Expectation Conflict.

H5: There is significant difference between the age group and stress factor Role Erosion.

Ho: There is no significant difference between the age group and stress factor Role Erosion.

ANOVA					
RE_TOTAL					
	Sum of Squares	*df*	*Mean Square*	*F*	*Sig.*
Between Groups	139.84	12	11.65	.79	.65
Within Groups	1676.39	115	14.57		
Total	**1816.24**	**127**			

Interpretation: here significant value is 0.65 which is greater than 0.05. So null hypothesis is accepted which says there is no significant difference between age group and Role Erosion.

H6: There is significant difference between the age group and stress factor Role Overload.

Ho: There is no significant difference between the age group and stress factor Role Overload.

ANOVA					
RO_TOTAL					
	Sum of Squares	*Df*	*Mean Square*	*F*	*Sig.*
Between Groups	320.89	12	26.74	1.16	.31
Within Groups	2638.09	115	22.94		
Total	**2958.99**	**127**			

Interpretation: here significant value is 0.31 which is greater than 0.05. So null hypothesis is accepted which says there is no significant difference between age group and Role Overload.

H7: There is significant difference between the age group and stress factor Role Isolation.

Ho: There is no significant difference between the age group and stress factor Role Isolation.

ANOVA					
RI TOTAL					
	Sum of Squares	*df*	*Mean Square*	*F*	*Sig.*
Between Groups	121.44	12	10.12	.68	.76
Within Groups	1703.77	115	14.81		
Total	**1825.21**	**127**			

Interpretation: here significant value is 0.765 which is greater than 0.05. So null hypothesis is accepted which says there is no significant difference between age group and Role Isolation.

H8: There is significant difference between the age group and stress factor Personal lnadequacy.

Ho: There is no significant difference between the age group and stress factor Personal lnadequacy.

ANOVA					
Pin TOTAL					
	Sum of Squares	*df*	*Mean Square*	*F*	*Sig.*
Between Groups	142.69	12	11.89	.84	.60
Within Groups	1628.27	115	14.15		
Total	**1770.96**	**127**			

Interpretation: here significant value is 0.60 which is greater than 0.05. So null hypothesis is accepted which says there is no significant difference between age group and Personal lnadequacy.

H9: There is significant difference between the age group and stress factor Self Role Distance.

Ho: There is no significant difference between the age group and stress factor Self Role Distance.

ANOVA					
PIn_TOTAL					
	Sum of Squares	***df***	***Mean Square***	***F***	***Sig.***
Between Groups	142.69	12	11.89	.84	.60
Within Groups	1628.27	115	14.15		
Total	**1770.96**	**127**			

Interpretation: here significant value is 0.15 which is greater than 0.05. So null hypothesis is accepted which says there is no significant difference between age group and Self Role Distance.

H10: There is significant difference between the age group and stress factor Role Ambiguity.

Ho: There is no significant difference between the age group and stress factor Role Ambiguity.

ANOVA					
RA TOTAL					
	Sum of Squares	***Df***	***Mean Square***	***F***	***Sig.***
Between Groups	182.88	12	15.24	1.14	.33
Within Groups	1527.484	115	13.282		
Total	**1710.367**	**127**			

Interpretation: here significant value is 0.33 which is greater than 0.05. So null hypothesis is accepted which says there is no significant difference between age group and Role Ambiguity.

H11: There is significant difference between the age group and stress factor Role Inadequacy.

Ho: There is no significant difference between the age group and stress factor Role Inadequacy.

ANOVA					
RIN TOTAL					
	Sum of Squares	*df*	*Mean Square*	*F*	*Sig.*
Between Groups	251.95	12	20.99	1.05	.40
Within Groups	2281.91	115	19.84		
Total	**2533.87**	**127**			

Interpretation: here significant value is 0.40 which is greater than 0.05. So null hypothesis is accepted which says there is no significant difference between age group and Role Inadequacy.

TEST: 4 ANOVA to personality

H12: There is significant difference between the age group and Agreeableness.

Ho: There is no significant difference between the age group and Agreeableness.

ANOVA					
Agreeableness					
	Sum of Squares	*df*	*Mean Square*	*F*	*Sig.*
Between Groups	948.87	12	79.07	.82	.62
Within Groups	10859.93	113	96.10		
Total	**11808.80**	**125**			

Interpretation: here significant value is 0.62 which is greater than 0.05. So null hypothesis is accepted which says there is no significant difference between age group and Agreeableness.

H13: There is significant difference between the age group and Sociability.

Ho: There is no significant difference between the age group and Sociability.

ANOVA					
Sociability					
	Sum of Squares	*df*	*Mean Square*	*F*	*Sig.*
Between Groups	452.74	12	37.72	.90	.54
Within Groups	4776.72	115	41.53		
Total	**5229.46**	**127**			

Interpretation: here significant value is 0.54 which is greater than 0.05. So null hypothesis is accepted which says there is no significant difference between age group and sociability.

H14: There is significant difference between the age group and Openness to experience.

Ho: There is no significant difference between the age group and Openness to experience.

ANOVA					
Openness					
	Sum of Squares	*df*	*Mean Square*	*F*	*Sig.*
Between Groups	917.53	12	76.46	.96	.48
Within Groups	9072.76	115	78.89		
Total	**9990.30**	**127**			

Interpretation: here significant value is 0.48 which is greater than 0.05. So null hypothesis is accepted which says there is no significant difference between age group and Openness to experience.

H15: There is significant difference between the age group and Extraversion.

Ho: There is no significant difference between the age group and Extraversion.

ANOVA					
Extraversion					
	Sum of Squares	***df***	***Mean Square***	***F***	***Sig.***
Between Groups	461.56	12	38.46	.42	.94
Within Groups	10333.93	115	89.86		
Total	**10795.50**	**127**			

Interpretation: here significant value is 0.94 which is greater than 0.05. So null hypothesis is accepted which says there is no significant difference between age group and Extraversion.

H16: There is significant difference between the age group and Conscientiousness.

Ho: There is no significant difference between the age group and Conscientiousness.

ANOVA					
Conscientiousness					
	Sum of Squares	***df***	***Mean Square***	***F***	***Sig.***
Between Groups	655.80	12	54.65	.60	.83
Within Groups	10411.63	115	90.53		
Total	**11067.43**	**127**			

Interpretation: here significant value is 0.83 which is greater than 0.05. So null hypothesis is accepted which says there is no significant difference between age group and conscientiousness.

TEST: 5 There are two different category of people having different profiles.

Anova: Two-Factor With Replication

Summary	*IRD Total*	*RS Total*	*REC Total*	*RE Total*	*RO Total*	*RI Total*	*PIN Total*	*SRD Total*	*RA Total*	*RIN Total*	*Total*
1											
Count	23	23	23	23	23	23	23	23	23	23	230
Sum	204	177	137	210	141	176	190	141	144	155	1675
Average	8.86	7.69	5.95	9.13	6.13	7.65	8.26	6.13	6.26	6.73913	7.282609
Variance	8.66	11.13	18.58	21.30	23.66	21.96	16.74	16.02	19.38	17.3834	18.09882
2											
Count	23	23	23	23	23	23	23	23	23	23	230
Sum	138	101	143	190	76	150	140	85	73	103	1199
Average	6	4.39	6.21	8.26	3.30	6.52	6.08	3.69	3.17	4.478261	5.213043
Variance	14.18	8.24	10.72	12.20	9.31	7.98	11.53	8.13	7.24	16.71542	12.69241
Total											
Count		46	46	46	46	46	46	46	46	46	46
Sum		342	278	280	400	217	326	330	226	217	258
Average		7.43	6.04	6.08	8.69	4.71	7.08	7.17	4.91	4.71	5.608696
Variance		13.27	12.26	14.34	16.57	18.16	14.97	15.03	13.32	15.45	17.97681

ANOVA

Source of Variation	*SS*	*df*	*MS*	*F*	*P-value*	*F crit*
Sample	492.55	1	492.55	35.04	6.51E-09	3.86
Columns	731.61	9	81.29	5.78	1.29E-07	1.90
Interaction	134.61	9	14.95	1.064	0.388	1.90
Within	6184.95	440	14.05			
Total	**7543.74**	**459**				

Anova two-factor with replication is applied to test whether there is any difference in the Stress levels of these two category of people i.e. Call Receivers and Outreach Counsellors. Call receivers are the employees who work at GVK EMRI. Their work is to answer the emergency calls, enter the required data, inform and coordinate with the outreach counsellors and send the emergency vehicle whenever required. And outreach counsellors are majorly responsible to reuse the victims within couple of minutes to handle the situation. Because the work of both the categories of people differ, ANOVA was applied to check the difference between their stress levels.

To determine whether any of the differences between the means are statistically significant, p-value was compared to the significance level to assess the null hypothesis. Here the p value of Sample is 6.51E-09 which is less than 0.05 which means there is significant difference between the stress levels of both the samples working on different profiles.

Also, the p-value between columns is 1.29E-07 which is again less than 0.05 which means there is significant difference in the levels of stress relating to different dimensions among the respondents.

Here the p-value of Sample is 6.51E-09 which is less than 0.05 which means there is significant difference between the stress levels of both the samples working on different profiles.

Also, the p value between columns is 1.29E-07 which is again less than 0.05 which means there is significant difference in the levels of stress relating to different dimensions among the respondents.

TEST: 5

A chi-square test statistical hypothesis test, was used wherein the sampling distribution of the test statistic is a chi-square distribution when the null hypothesis is true. Without other qualification, 'chi-square test' was also used for Pearson's chi-square test. The chi-square test was used to determine whether there is a significant difference between the expected frequencies and the observed frequencies in one or more categories.

In the standard applications of the test, the observations were classified, and the null hypothesis was considered, to obtain the probability of any observation falling into the corresponding class. The purpose of the test is to evaluate how likely it is between the observations and the null hypothesis.

Chi-square test was constructed from a sum of squared errors and the sample variance. Test statistics that follow a chi-square distribution arose from an assumption of independent normally distributed data, which is valid in many cases due to the central limit theorem. Also the sampling distribution (if the null hypothesis is true) can be made to approximate a chi-square distribution as closely as desired by making the sample size large enough. Therefore, dependence of every stress factor on each personality type was calculated.

To check the dependence of individual stress dimension with individual personality type.

Inter Role Distance and Adjustment

H17: Inter Role Distance and Adjustment factors are dependent of each other.

Ho: Inter Role Distance and Adjustment factors are independent of each other.

Chi-Square Tests

	Value	*Df*	*Asymp. Sig. (2-sided)*
Pearson Chi-Square	284.28[a]	234	.01
Likelihood Ratio	175.44	234	.99
Linear-by-Linear Association	.47	1	.48
N of Valid Cases	127		

a. 265 cells (99.6 %) have expected count less than 5. The minimum expected count is .01.

Interpretation: here significant value is 0.01 which is smaller than 0.05. So null hypothesis is rejected and alternate is accepted. This means that Inter Role Distance and Adjustment factors are dependent of each other.

Inter Role Distance and Sociability

H18: Inter Role Distance and Sociability factors are dependent of each other.

Ho: Inter Role Distance and Sociability factors are independent of each other.

Chi-Square Tests			
	Value	*df*	*Asymp. Sig. (2-sided)*
Pearson Chi-Square	225.01[a]	216	.32
Likelihood Ratio	181.06	216	.96
Linear-by-Linear Association	.65	1	.41
N of Valid Cases	129		
a. 247 cells (100.0%) have expected count less than 5. The minimum expected count is .01.			

Interpretation: here significant value is 0.32 which is greater than 0.05. So null hypothesis is accepted. This means that Inter Role Distance and Sociability are independent of each other.

Inter Role Distance and Openness to Experience

H19: Inter Role Distance and Openness to Experience factors are dependent of each other.

Ho: Inter Role Distance and Openness to Experience factors are independent of each other.

Chi-Square Tests			
	Value	*df*	*Asymp. Sig. (2-sided)*
Pearson Chi-Square	396.11[a]	252	.00
Likelihood Ratio	233.00	252	.79
Linear-by-Linear Association	1.32	1	.25
N of Valid Cases	129		
a. 285 cells (100.0%) have expected count less than 5. The minimum expected count is .01.			

Interpretation: here significant value is 0.00 which is smaller than 0.05. So null hypothesis is rejected and alternate is accepted. This means that Inter Role Distance and Openness to Experience factors are dependent of each other.

Inter Role Distance and Agreeableness

H20: Inter Role Distance and Agreeableness factors are dependent of each other.

Ho: Inter Role Distance and Agreeableness factors are independent of each other.

Chi-Square Tests			
	Value	*df*	*Asymp. Sig. (2-sided)*
Pearson Chi-Square	350.16[a]	234	.00
Likelihood Ratio	193.61	234	.97
Linear-by-Linear Association	1.31	1	.25
N of Valid Cases	129		
a. 266 cells (100.0%) have expected count less than 5. The minimum expected count is .01.			

Interpretation: here significant value is 0.00 which is smaller than 0.05. So null hypothesis is rejected and alternate is accepted. This means that Inter Role Distance and Agreeableness factors are dependent of each other

Inter Role Distance and Conscientiousness

H21: Inter Role Distance and Conscientiousness factors are dependent of each other.

Ho: Inter Role Distance and Conscientiousness factors are independent of each other.

Chi-Square Tests			
	Value	*df*	*Asymp. Sig. (2-sided)*
Pearson Chi-Square	366.07[a]	306	.01
Likelihood Ratio	250.38	306	.99
Linear-by-Linear Association	.03	1	.85
N of Valid Cases	129		
a. 342 cells (100.0%) have expected count less than 5. The minimum expected count is .01.			

Interpretation: here significant value is 0.01 which is smaller than 0.05. So null hypothesis is rejected and alternate is accepted. This means that Inter Role Distance and Conscientiousness factors are dependent of each other.

Role Stagnation and Adjustment

H22: Role Stagnation and Adjustment factors are dependent of each other.

Ho: Role Stagnation and Adjustment factors are independent of each other.

Chi-Square Tests			
	Value	*df*	*Asymp. Sig. (2-sided)*
Pearson Chi-Square	246.62[a]	221	.11
Likelihood Ratio	192.12	221	.92
Linear-by-Linear Association	.18	1	.67
N of Valid Cases	127		
a. 251 cells (99.6%) have expected count less than 5. The minimum expected count is .01.			

Interpretation: here significant value is 0.11 which is greater than 0.05. So null hypothesis is accepted. This means that Role Stagnation and Adjustment factors are independent of each other.

Role Stagnation and Sociability

H23: Role Stagnation and Sociability factors are dependent of each other.

Ho: Role Stagnation and Sociability factors are independent of each other.

Chi-Square Tests			
	Value	*df*	*Asymp. Sig. (2-sided)*
Pearson Chi-Square	227.86[a]	204	.12
Likelihood Ratio	175.92	204	.92
Linear-by-Linear Association	.69	1	.40
N of Valid Cases	129		
a. 234 cells (100.0%) have expected count less than 5. The minimum expected count is .01.			

Interpretation: here significant value is 0.12 which is greater than 0.05. So null hypothesis is accepted. This means that Role Stagnation and Sociability factors are independent of each other.

Role Stagnation and Openness to Experience

H24: Role Stagnation and Openness to Experience factors are dependent of each other.

Ho: Role Stagnation and Openness to Experience factors are independent of each other.

Chi-Square Tests			
	Value	*df*	*Asymp. Sig. (2-sided)*
Pearson Chi-Square	282.59[a]	238	.02
Likelihood Ratio	203.54	238	.94
Linear-by-Linear Association	1.10	1	.29
N of Valid Cases	129		
a. 270 cells (100.0%) have expected count less than 5. The minimum expected count is .01.			

Interpretation: here significant value is 0.02 which is smaller than 0.05. So null hypothesis is rejected and alternate is accepted. This means that Role Stagnation and Openness to Experience factors are dependent of each other.

Role Stagnation and Agreeableness

H25: Role Stagnation and Agreeableness factors are dependent of each other.

Ho: Role Stagnation and Agreeableness factors are independent of each other.

Chi-Square Tests			
	Value	*df*	*Asymp. Sig. (2-sided)*
Pearson Chi-Square	244.53[a]	221	.13
Likelihood Ratio	191.00	221	.92
Linear-by-Linear Association	2.65	1	.10
N of Valid Cases	129		
a. 252 cells (100.0%) have expected count less than 5. The minimum expected count is .01.			

Interpretation: here significant value is 0.13 which is greater than 0.05. So null hypothesis is accepted. This means that Role Stagnation and Agreeableness factors are independent of each other.

Role Stagnation and Conscientiousness

H26: Role Stagnation and Conscientiousness factors are dependent of each other.

Ho: Role Stagnation and Conscientiousness factors are independent of each other.

Chi-Square Tests			
	Value	*df*	*Asymp. Sig. (2-sided)*
Pearson Chi-Square	354.06[a]	289	.00
Likelihood Ratio	217.27	289	.99
Linear-by-Linear Association	1.85	1	.17
N of Valid Cases	129		
a. 324 cells (100.0%) have expected count less than 5. The minimum expected count is .01.			

Interpretation: here significant value is 0.00 which is smaller than 0.05. So null hypothesis is rejected and alternate is accepted. This means that Role Stagnation and Conscientiousness factors are dependent of each other.

Role Expectation Conflict and Adjustment

H27: Role Expectation Conflict and Adjustment factors are dependent of each other.

Ho: Role Expectation Conflict and Adjustment factors are independent of each other.

Chi-Square Tests			
	Value	*Df*	*Asymp. Sig. (2-sided)*
Pearson Chi-Square	204.65[a]	182	.12
Likelihood Ratio	166.90	182	.78
Linear-by-Linear Association	.04	1	.83
N of Valid Cases	127		
a. 210 cells (100.0%) have expected count less than 5. The minimum expected count is .01.			

Interpretation: here significant value is 0.12 which is greater than 0.05. So null hypothesis is accepted. This means that Role Expectation Conflict and Adjustment factors are independent of each other.

Role Expectation Conflict and Sociability

H28: Role Expectation Conflict and Sociability factors are dependent of each other.

Ho: Role Expectation Conflict and Sociability factors are independent of each other.

Chi-Square Tests			
	Value	*Df*	*Asymp. Sig. (2-sided)*
Pearson Chi-Square	214.26[a]	180	.04
Likelihood Ratio	170.66	180	.67
Linear-by-Linear Association	.02	1	.86
N of Valid Cases	129		
a. 208 cells (100.0%) have expected count less than 5. The minimum expected count is .01.			

Interpretation: here significant value is 0.04 which is smaller than 0.05. So null hypothesis is rejected and alternate is accepted. This means that Role Expectation Conflict and Sociability factors are dependent of each other.

Role Expectation Conflict and Openness to Experience

H29: Role Expectation Conflict and Openness to Experience factors are dependent of each other.

Ho: Role Expectation Conflict and Openness to Experience factors are independent of each other.

Chi-Square Tests			
	Value	*df*	*Asymp. Sig. (2-sided)*
Pearson Chi-Square	360.97[a]	210	.00
Likelihood Ratio	172.50	210	.97
Linear-by-Linear Association	.28	1	.59
N of Valid Cases	129		
a. 240 cells (100.0%) have expected count less than 5. The minimum expected count is .01.			

Interpretation: here significant value is 0.000 which is smaller than 0.05. So null hypothesis is rejected and alternate is accepted. This means that Role Expectation Conflict and Openness to Experience factors are dependent of each other.

Role Expectation Conflict and Agreeableness

H30: Role Expectation Conflict and Agreeableness factors are dependent of each other.

Ho: Role Expectation Conflict and Agreeableness factors are independent of each other.

Chi-Square Tests			
	Value	*df*	*Asymp. Sig. (2-sided)*
Pearson Chi-Square	180.98[a]	195	.75
Likelihood Ratio	153.39	195	.98
Linear-by-Linear Association	1.10	1	.29
N of Valid Cases	129		

a. 224 cells (100.0%) have expected count less than 5. The minimum expected count is .01.

Interpretation: here significant value is 0.76 which is greater than 0.05. So null hypothesis is accepted. This means that Role Expectation Conflict and Agreeableness factors are independent of each other.

Role Expectation Conflict and Conscientiousness

H31: Role Expectation Conflict and Conscientiousness factors are dependent of each other.

Ho: Role Expectation Conflict and Conscientiousness factors are independent of each other.

Chi-Square Tests			
	Value	*df*	*Asymp. Sig. (2-sided)*
Pearson Chi-Square	287.53[a]	255	.07
Likelihood Ratio	232.34	255	.84
Linear-by-Linear Association	.39	1	.53
N of Valid Cases	129		
a. 288 cells (100.0%) have expected count less than 5. The minimum expected count is .01.			

Interpretation: here significant value is 0.07 which is greater than 0.05. So null hypothesis is accepted. This means that Role Expectation Conflict and Conscientiousness factors are independent of each other.

Role Erosion and Adjustment

H32: Role Erosion and Adjustment factors are dependent of each other.

Ho: Role Erosion and Adjustment factors are independent of each other.

Chi-Square Tests			
	Value	*df*	*Asymp. Sig. (2-sided)*
Pearson Chi-Square	260.00[a]	208	.00
Likelihood Ratio	175.24	208	.95
Linear-by-Linear Association	.43	1	.50
N of Valid Cases	127		
a. 237 cells (99.6%) have expected count less than 5. The minimum expected count is .01.			

Interpretation: here significant value is 0.00 which is smaller than 0.05. So null hypothesis is rejected and alternate is accepted. This means that Role Erosion and Adjustment factors are dependent of each other.

Role Erosion and Sociability

H33: Role Erosion and Sociability factors are dependent of each other.

Ho: Role Erosion and Sociability factors are independent of each other.

Chi-Square Tests			
	Value	*df*	*Asymp. Sig. (2-sided)*
Pearson Chi-Square	241.22[a]	192	.00
Likelihood Ratio	165.53	192	.91
Linear-by-Linear Association	1.20	1	.27
N of Valid Cases	129		
a. 221 cells (100.0%) have expected count less than 5. The minimum expected count is .01.			

Interpretation: here significant value is 0.00 which is smaller than 0.05. So null hypothesis is rejected and alternate is accepted. This means that Role Erosion and Sociability factors are dependent of each other.

Role Erosion and Openness to Experience

H34: Role Erosion and Openness to Experience factors are dependent of each other.

Ho: Role Erosion and Openness to Experience factors are independent of each other.

Chi-Square Tests

	Value	*df*	*Asymp. Sig. (2-sided)*
Pearson Chi-Square	259.65[a]	224	.05
Likelihood Ratio	187.42	224	.96
Linear-by-Linear Association	.39	1	.52
N of Valid Cases	129		
a. 255 cells (100.0%) have expected count less than 5. The minimum expected count is .01.			

Interpretation: here significant value is 0.05 which is greater than 0.05. So null hypothesis is accepted. This means that Role Erosion and Openness to Experience factors are independent of each other.

Role Erosion and Agreeableness

H35: Role Erosion and Agreeableness factors are dependent of each other.

Ho: Role Erosion and Agreeableness factors are independent of each other.

Chi-Square Tests

	Value	*df*	*Asymp. Sig. (2-sided)*
Pearson Chi-Square	234.77[a]	208	.09
Likelihood Ratio	187.99	208	.83
Linear-by-Linear Association	.04	1	.82
N of Valid Cases	129		
a. 238 cells (100.0%) have expected count less than 5. The minimum expected count is .01.			

Interpretation: here significant value is 0.09 which is greater than 0.05. So null hypothesis is accepted. This means that Role Erosion and Agreeableness factors are independent of each other.

Role Erosion and Conscientiousness

H36: Role Erosion and Conscientiousness factors are dependent of each other.

Ho: Role Erosion and Conscientiousness factors are independent of each other.

Chi-Square Tests			
	Value	*df*	*Asymp. Sig. (2-sided)*
Pearson Chi-Square	320.08[a]	272	.02
Likelihood Ratio	199.12	272	1.00
Linear-by-Linear Association	.00	1	.96
N of Valid Cases	129		
a. 306 cells (100.0%) have expected count less than 5. The minimum expected count is .01.			

Interpretation: here significant value is 0.02 which is smaller than 0.05. So null hypothesis is rejected and alternate is accepted. This means that Role Erosion and Conscientiousness factors are dependent of each other.

Role Overload and Adjustment

H37: Role Overload and Adjustment factors are dependent of each other.

Ho: Role Overload and Adjustment factors are independent of each other.

Chi-Square Tests			
	Value	*df*	*Asymp. Sig. (2-sided)*
Pearson Chi-Square	377.34[a]	221	.00
Likelihood Ratio	174.04	221	.99
Linear-by-Linear Association	.219	1	.64
N of Valid Cases	127		
a. 251 cells (99.6%) have expected count less than 5. The minimum expected count is .01.			

Interpretation: here significant value is 0.00 which is smaller than 0.05. So null hypothesis is rejected and alternate is accepted. This means that Role Overload and Adjustment factors are dependent of each other.

Role Overload and Sociability

H38: Role Overload and Sociability factors are dependent of each other.

Ho: Role Overload and Sociability factors are independent of each other.

Chi-Square Tests			
	Value	*df*	*Asymp. Sig. (2-sided)*
Pearson Chi-Square	223.73[a]	204	.16
Likelihood Ratio	172.29	204	.94
Linear-by-Linear Association	1.23	1	.26
N of Valid Cases	129		
a. 234 cells (100.0%) have expected count less than 5. The minimum expected count is .01.			

Interpretation: here significant value is 0.16 which is greater than 0.05. So null hypothesis is accepted. This means that Role Overload and Sociability factors are independent of each other.

Role Overload and Openness to Experience

H39: Role Overload and Openness to Experience factors are dependent of each other.

Ho: Role Overload and Openness to Experience factors are independent of each other.

Chi-Square Tests			
	Value	*df*	*Asymp. Sig. (2-sided)*
Pearson Chi-Square	304.60[a]	238	.00
Likelihood Ratio	175.54	238	.99
Linear-by-Linear Association	3.18	1	.07
N of Valid Cases	129		
a. 270 cells (100.0%) have expected count less than 5. The minimum expected count is .01.			

Interpretation: here significant value is 0.00 which is smaller than 0.05. So null hypothesis is rejected and alternate is accepted. This means that Role Overload and Openness to Experience factors are dependent of each other.

Role Overload and Agreeableness

H40: Role Overload and Agreeableness factors are dependent of each other.

Ho: Role Overload and Agreeableness factors are independent of each other.

Chi-Square Tests			
	Value	*df*	*Asymp. Sig. (2-sided)*
Pearson Chi-Square	288.71[a]	221	.00
Likelihood Ratio	193.82	221	.90
Linear-by-Linear Association	.18	1	.66
N of Valid Cases	129		
a. 252 cells (100.0%) have expected count less than 5. The minimum expected count is .01.			

Interpretation: here significant value is 0.00 which is smaller than 0.05. So null hypothesis is rejected and alternate is accepted. This means that Role Overload and Agreeableness factors are dependent of each other.

Role Overload and Conscientiousness

H41: Role Overload and Conscientiousness factors are dependent of each other.

Ho: Role Overload and Conscientiousness factors are independent of each other.

Chi-Square Tests			
	Value	*df*	*Asymp. Sig. (2-sided)*
Pearson Chi-Square	403.89[a]	289	.00
Likelihood Ratio	214.06	289	1.00
Linear-by-Linear Association	3.79	1	.05
N of Valid Cases	129		
a. 324 cells (100.0%) have expected count less than 5. The minimum expected count is .01.			

Interpretation: here significant value is 0.00 which is smaller than 0.05. So null hypothesis is rejected and alternate is accepted. This means that Role Overload and Conscientiousness factors are dependent of each other.

Role Isolation and Adjustment

H42: Role Isolation and Adjustment factors are dependent of each other.

Ho: Role Isolation and Adjustment factors are independent of each other.

Chi-Square Tests			
	Value	*df*	*Asymp. Sig. (2-sided)*
Pearson Chi-Square	205.92[a]	208	.52
Likelihood Ratio	167.78	208	.98
Linear-by-Linear Association	.00	1	.94
N of Valid Cases	127		
a. 238 cells (100.0%) have expected count less than 5. The minimum expected count is .01.			

Interpretation: here significant value is 0.52 which is greater than 0.05. So null hypothesis is accepted. This means that Role Isolation and Adjustment factors are independent of each other.

Role Isolation and Sociability

H43: Role Isolation and Sociability factors are dependent of each other.

Ho: Role Isolation and Sociability factors are independent of each other.

Chi-Square Tests			
	Value	*df*	*Asymp. Sig. (2-sided)*
Pearson Chi-Square	222.68[a]	192	.06
Likelihood Ratio	178.40	192	.75
Linear-by-Linear Association	.21	1	.64
N of Valid Cases	129		
a. 221 cells (100.0%) have expected count less than 5. The minimum expected count is .01.			

Interpretation: here significant value is 0.06 which is greater than 0.05. So null hypothesis is accepted. This means that Role Isolation and Sociability factors are independent of each other.

Role Isolation and Openness to Experience

H44: Role Isolation and Openness to Experience factors are dependent of each other.

Ho: Role Isolation and Openness to Experience factors are independent of each other.

Chi-Square Tests			
	Value	*df*	*Asymp. Sig. (2-sided)*
Pearson Chi-Square	230.61[a]	224	.36
Likelihood Ratio	184.29	224	.97
Linear-by-Linear Association	.86	1	.35
N of Valid Cases	129		
a. 255 cells (100.0%) have expected count less than 5. The minimum expected count is .01.			

Interpretation: here significant value is 0.36 which is greater than 0.05. So null hypothesis is accepted. This means that Role Isolation and Openness to Experience factors are independent of each other.

Role Isolation and Agreeableness

H45: Role Isolation and Agreeableness factors are dependent of each other

Ho: Role Isolation and Agreeableness factors are independent of each other.

Chi-Square Tests			
	Value	*df*	*Asymp. Sig. (2-sided)*
Pearson Chi-Square	275.29[a]	208	.00
Likelihood Ratio	190.54	208	.80
Linear-by-Linear Association	.02	1	.87
N of Valid Cases	129		
a. 238 cells (100.0%) have expected count less than 5. The minimum expected count is .01.			

Interpretation: here significant value is 0.00 which is smaller than 0.05. So null hypothesis is rejected and alternate is accepted. This means that Role Isolation and Agreeableness factors are dependent of each other.

Role Isolation and Conscientiousness

H46: Role Isolation and Conscientiousness factors are dependent of each other.

Ho: Role Isolation and Conscientiousness factors are independent of each other.

Chi-Square Tests			
	Value	*df*	*Asymp. Sig. (2-sided)*
Pearson Chi-Square	341.86[a]	272	.00
Likelihood Ratio	220.71	272	.99
Linear-by-Linear Association	.11	1	.73
N of Valid Cases	129		
a. 306 cells (100.0%) have expected count less than 5. The minimum expected count is .01.			

Interpretation: here significant value is 0.003 which is smaller than 0.05. So null hypothesis is rejected and alternate is accepted. This means that Role Isolation and Conscientiousness factors are dependent of each other.

Planning Inadequacy and Adjustment

H47: Planning Inadequacy and Adjustment factors are dependent of each other.

Ho: Planning Inadequacy and Adjustment factors are independent of each other.

Chi-Square Tests			
	Value	*df*	*Asymp. Sig. (2-sided)*
Pearson Chi-Square	263.07[a]	195	.00
Likelihood Ratio	176.55	195	.82
Linear-by-Linear Association	.00	1	.92
N of Valid Cases	127		
a. 223 cells (99.6%) have expected count less than 5. The minimum expected count is .01.			

Interpretation: here significant value is 0.00 which is smaller than 0.05. So null hypothesis is rejected and alternate is accepted. This means that Planning Inadequacy and Adjustment factors are dependent of each other.

Planning Inadequacy and Sociability

H48: Planning Inadequacy and Sociability factors are dependent of each other.

Ho: Planning Inadequacy and Sociability factors are independent of each other.

Chi-Square Tests			
	Value	*df*	*Asymp. Sig. (2-sided)*
Pearson Chi-Square	196.29[a]	180	.19
Likelihood Ratio	162.01	180	.82
Linear-by-Linear Association	.36	1	.54
N of Valid Cases	129		
a. 208 cells (100.0%) have expected count less than 5. The minimum expected count is .02.			

Interpretation: here significant value is 0.19 which is greater than 0.05. So null hypothesis is accepted. This means that Planning Inadequacy and Sociability factors are independent of each other.

Planning Inadequacy and Openness to Experience

H49: Planning Inadequacy and Openness to Experience factors are dependent of each other.

Ho: Planning Inadequacy and Openness to Experience factors are independent of each other.

Chi-Square Tests			
	Value	*Df*	*Asymp. Sig. (2-sided)*
Pearson Chi-Square	272.74[a]	210	.00
Likelihood Ratio	180.68	210	.92
Linear-by-Linear Association	.01	1	.89
N of Valid Cases	129		
a. 240 cells (100.0%) have expected count less than 5. The minimum expected count is .02.			

Interpretation: here significant value is 0.00 which is smaller than 0.05. So null hypothesis is rejected and alternate is accepted. This means that Planning Inadequacy and Openness to Experience factors are dependent of each other.

Planning Inadequacy and Agreeableness

H50: Planning Inadequacy and Agreeableness factors are dependent of each other.

Ho: Planning Inadequacy and Agreeableness factors are independent of each other.

Chi-Square Tests			
	Value	*df*	*Asymp. Sig. (2-sided)*
Pearson Chi-Square	205.00[a]	195	.29
Likelihood Ratio	173.52	195	.86
Linear-by-Linear Association	.42	1	.51
N of Valid Cases	129		
a. 224 cells (100.0%) have expected count less than 5. The minimum expected count is .02.			

Interpretation: here significant value is 0.29 which is greater than 0.05. So null hypothesis is accepted. This means that Planning Inadequacy and Agreeableness factors are independent of each other.

Planning Inadequacy and Conscientiousness

H51: Planning Inadequacy and Conscientiousness factors are dependent of each other.

Ho: Planning Inadequacy and Conscientiousness factors are independent of each other.

Chi-Square Tests			
	Value	*df*	*Asymp. Sig. (2-sided)*
Pearson Chi-Square	267.92[a]	255	.27
Likelihood Ratio	203.24	255	.99
Linear-by-Linear Association	.08	1	.77
N of Valid Cases	129		
a. 288 cells (100.0%) have expected count less than 5. The minimum expected count is .02.			

Interpretation: here significant value is 0.22 which is greater than 0.05. So null hypothesis is accepted. This means that Planning Inadequacy and Conscientiousness factors are independent of each other.

Self-Role Distance and Adjustment

H52: Self Role Distance and Adjustment factors are dependent of each other.

Ho: Self Role Distance and Adjustment factors are independent of each other.

Chi-Square Tests			
	Value	*Df*	*Asymp. Sig. (2-sided)*
Pearson Chi-Square	328.81[a]	195	.00
Likelihood Ratio	174.96	195	.84
Linear-by-Linear Association	.03	1	.84
N of Valid Cases	127		
a. 223 cells (99.6%) have expected count less than 5. The minimum expected count is .01.			

Interpretation: here significant value is 0.00 which is smaller than 0.05. So null hypothesis is rejected and alternate is accepted. This means that Self Role Distance and Adjustment factors are dependent of each other.

Self-Role Distance and Sociability

H53: Self Role Distance and Sociability factors are dependent of each other.

Ho: Self Role Distance and Sociability factors are independent of each other.

Chi-Square Tests			
	Value	*df*	*Asymp. Sig. (2-sided)*
Pearson Chi-Square	215.01[a]	180	.03
Likelihood Ratio	161.50	180	.83
Linear-by-Linear Association	.62	1	.43
N of Valid Cases	129		
a. 208 cells (100.0%) have expected count less than 5. The minimum expected count is .01.			

Interpretation: here significant value is 0.03 which is smaller than 0.05. So null hypothesis is rejected and alternate is accepted. This means that Self Role Distance and Sociability factors are dependent of each other.

Self-Role Distance and Openness to Experience

H54: Self Role Distance and Openness to Experience factors are dependent of each other.

Ho: Self Role Distance and Openness to Experience factors are independent of each other.

Chi-Square Tests			
	Value	*df*	*Asymp. Sig. (2-sided)*
Pearson Chi-Square	228.42[a]	210	.18
Likelihood Ratio	161.35	210	.99
Linear-by-Linear Association	.00	1	.97
N of Valid Cases	129		
a. 240 cells (100.0%) have expected count less than 5. The minimum expected count is .01.			

Interpretation: here significant value is 0.18 which is greater than 0.05. So null hypothesis is accepted. This means that Self Role Distance and Openness to Experience factors are independent of each other.

Self-Role Distance and Agreeableness

H55: Self Role Distance and Agreeableness factors are dependent of each other.

Ho: Self Role Distance and Agreeableness factors are independent of each other.

Chi-Square Tests			
	Value	***df***	***Asymp. Sig. (2-sided)***
Pearson Chi-Square	218.89[a]	195	.11
Likelihood Ratio	172.68	195	.87
Linear-by-Linear Association	.93	1	.33
N of Valid Cases	129		
a. 224 cells (100.0%) have expected count less than 5. The minimum expected count is .01.			

Interpretation: here significant value is 0.11 which is greater than 0.05. So null hypothesis is accepted. This means that Self Role Distance and Agreeableness factors are independent of each other.

Self-Role Distance and Conscientiousness

H56: Self Role Distance and Conscientiousness factors are dependent of each other.

Ho: Self Role Distance and Conscientiousness factors are independent of each other.

Chi-Square Tests			
	Value	***df***	***Asymp. Sig. (2-sided)***
Pearson Chi-Square	310.35[a]	255	.01
Likelihood Ratio	189.59	255	.99
Linear-by-Linear Association	1.45	1	.22
N of Valid Cases	129		
a. 288 cells (100.0%) have expected count less than 5. The minimum expected count is .01.			

Interpretation: here significant value is 0.01 which is smaller than 0.05. So null hypothesis is rejected and alternate is accepted. This means that Self Role Distance and Conscientiousness factors are dependent of each other.

Role Ambiguity and Adjustment

H57: Role Ambiguity and Adjustment factors are dependent of each other.

Ho: Role Ambiguity and Adjustment factors are independent of each other.

Chi-Square Tests			
	Value	*df*	*Asymp. Sig. (2-sided)*
Pearson Chi-Square	204.23[a]	182	.12
Likelihood Ratio	152.71	182	.94
Linear-by-Linear Association	4.71	1	.03
N of Valid Cases	127		
a. 207 cells (98.6%) have expected count less than 5. The minimum expected count is .01.			

Interpretation: here significant value is 0.12 which is greater than 0.05. So null hypothesis is accepted. This means that Role Ambiguity and Adjustment factors are independent of each other.

Role Ambiguity and Sociability

H58: Role Ambiguity and Sociability factors are dependent of each other.

Ho: Role Ambiguity and Sociability factors are independent of each other.

Chi-Square Tests			
	Value	*df*	*Asymp. Sig. (2-sided)*
Pearson Chi-Square	197.73[a]	168	.05
Likelihood Ratio	149.98	168	.83
Linear-by-Linear Association	2.32	1	.12
N of Valid Cases	129		
a. 195 cells (100.0%) have expected count less than 5. The minimum expected count is .01.			

Interpretation: here significant value is 0.05 which is greater than 0.05. So null hypothesis is accepted. This means that Role Ambiguity and Sociability factors are independent of each other.

Role Ambiguity and Openness to Experience

H59: Role Ambiguity and Openness to Experience factors are dependent of each other.

Ho: Role Ambiguity and Openness to Experience factors are independent of each other.

Chi-Square Tests			
	Value	*df*	*Asymp. Sig. (2-sided)*
Pearson Chi-Square	208.62[a]	196	.25
Likelihood Ratio	175.21	196	.85
Linear-by-Linear Association	.00	1	.99
N of Valid Cases	129		
a. 225 cells (100.0%) have expected count less than 5. The minimum expected count is .01.			

Interpretation: here significant value is 0.25 which is greater than 0.05. So null hypothesis is accepted. This means that Role Ambiguity and Openness to Experience factors are independent of each other.

Role Ambiguity and Agreeableness

H60: Role Ambiguity and Agreeableness factors are dependent of each other.

Ho: Role Ambiguity and Agreeableness factors are independent of each other.

Chi-Square Tests			
	Value	*df*	*Asymp. Sig. (2-sided)*
Pearson Chi-Square	192.33[a]	182	.28
Likelihood Ratio	156.62	182	.91
Linear-by-Linear Association	1.22	1	.26
N of Valid Cases	129		
a. 210 cells (100.0%) have expected count less than 5. The minimum expected count is .01.			

Interpretation: here significant value is 0.28 which is greater than 0.05. So null hypothesis is accepted. This means that Role Ambiguity and Agreeableness factors are independent of each other.

Role Ambiguity and Conscientiousness

H61: Role Ambiguity and Conscientiousness factors are dependent of each other.

Ho: Role Ambiguity and Conscientiousness factors are independent of each other.

Chi-Square Tests			
	Value	*df*	*Asymp. Sig. (2-sided)*
Pearson Chi-Square	408.02[a]	238	.00
Likelihood Ratio	209.11	238	.91
Linear-by-Linear Association	4.64	1	.03
N of Valid Cases	129		
a. 270 cells (100.0%) have expected count less than 5. The minimum expected count is .01.			

Interpretation: here significant value is 0.00 which is smaller than 0.05. So null hypothesis is rejected and alternate is accepted. This means that Role Ambiguity and Conscientiousness factors are dependent of each other.

Role Inadequacy and Adjustment

H62: Role Inadequacy and Adjustment factors are dependent of each other.

Ho: Role Inadequacy and Adjustment factors are independent of each other.

Chi-Square Tests			
	Value	*df*	*Asymp. Sig. (2-sided)*
Pearson Chi-Square	355.52[a]	221	.00
Likelihood Ratio	197.65	221	.86
Linear-by-Linear Association	.51	1	.47
N of Valid Cases	127		
a. 251 cells (99.6%) have expected count less than 5. The minimum expected count is .01.			

Interpretation: here significant value is 0.00 which is smaller than 0.05. So null hypothesis is rejected and alternate is accepted. This means that Role Inadequacy and Adjustment factors are dependent of each other.

Role Inadequacy and Sociability

H63: Role Inadequacy and Sociability factors are dependent of each other.

Ho: Role Inadequacy and Sociability factors are independent of each other.

Chi-Square Tests			
	Value	*df*	*Asymp. Sig. (2-sided)*
Pearson Chi-Square	265.87[a]	204	.00
Likelihood Ratio	190.71	204	.73
Linear-by-Linear Association	2.15	1	.14
N of Valid Cases	129		
a. 234 cells (100.0%) have expected count less than 5. The minimum expected count is .01.			

Interpretation: here significant value is 0.00 which is smaller than 0.05. So null hypothesis is rejected and alternate is accepted. This means that Role Inadequacy and Sociability factors are dependent of each other.

Role Inadequacy and Openness to Experience

H64: Role Inadequacy and Openness to Experience factors are dependent of each other.

Ho: Role Inadequacy and Openness to Experience factors are independent of each other.

Chi-Square Tests			
	Value	*df*	*Asymp. Sig. (2-sided)*
Pearson Chi-Square	272.39[a]	238	.06
Likelihood Ratio	180.24	238	.99
Linear-by-Linear Association	.47	1	.49
N of Valid Cases	129		
a. 270 cells (100.0%) have expected count less than 5. The minimum expected count is .01.			

Interpretation: here significant value is 0.06 which is greater than 0.05. So null hypothesis is accepted. This means that Role Inadequacy and Openness to Experience factors are independent of each other.

Role Inadequacy and Agreeableness

H65: Role Inadequacy and Agreeableness factors are dependent of each other.

Ho: Role Inadequacy and Agreeableness factors are independent of each other.

Chi-Square Tests			
	Value	*df*	*Asymp. Sig. (2-sided)*
Pearson Chi-Square	230.06[a]	221	.32
Likelihood Ratio	177.44	221	.98
Linear-by-Linear Association	.39	1	.52
N of Valid Cases	129		
a. 252 cells (100.0%) have expected count less than 5. The minimum expected count is .01.			

Interpretation: here significant value is 0.32 which is greater than 0.05. So null hypothesis is accepted. This means that Role Inadequacy and Agreeableness factors are independent of each other

Role Inadequacy and Conscientiousness

H66: Role Inadequacy and Conscientiousness factors are dependent of each other.

Ho: Role Inadequacy and Conscientiousness factors are independent of each other.

Chi-Square Tests			
	Value	*df*	*Asymp. Sig. (2-sided)*
Pearson Chi-Square	336.39[a]	289	.02
Likelihood Ratio	219.20	289	.99
Linear-by-Linear Association	1.98	1	.15
N of Valid Cases	129		
a. 324 cells (100.0%) have expected count less than 5. The minimum expected count is .01.			

Interpretation: here significant value is 0.02 which is smaller than 0.05. So null hypothesis is rejected and alternate is accepted. This means that Role Inadequacy and Conscientiousness factors are dependent of each other.

12

DISCUSSION AND CONCLUSION

Stress Dimension/ Personality type	*Adjustment*	*Sociability*	*Openness to Experience*	*Agreeableness*	*Conscientiousness*
Inter Role Distance	Dependent	Independent	Dependent	Dependent	Dependent
Role Stagnation	Independent	Independent	Dependent	Independent	Independent
Role Expectation Conflict	Independent	Dependent	Dependent	Independent	Dependent
Role Erosion	Dependent	Dependent	Independent	Independent	Dependent
Role Overload	Dependent	Independent	Dependent	Dependent	Dependent
Role Isolation	Independent	Independent	Independent	Dependent	Dependent
Personal Inadequacy	Dependent	Independent	Dependent	Independent	Independent
Self Role Distance	Dependent	Dependent	Independent	Independent	Dependent
Role Ambiguity	Independent	Independent	Independent	Independent	Dependent
Role Inadequacy	Dependent	Dependent	Independent	Independent	Dependent

The tests conducted above, revealed which organisational stress scale factors were dependent or independent of each type of personality type of the employees of the organisation. The results revealed that the organisational stress factor-Inter Role Distance had the highest dependency with the personality type of the employees. When an individual occupies more than one role there are bound to be conflicts between them. And with individuals occupying multiple roles in various groups inter role conflicts are quite common this also concludes that this is because of the Adjustment, Openness to change, Agreeableness and Conscientiousness factors of the individual's personality type.

Also, the organisational role scale factor-Role Overload had the highest dependency with the personality type of the employees. Too much of expectations from an individual by significant others in the role set leads to role overload. It is more likely to occur where role occupants lack power and there are large variations in the expected output and when delegation or assistance cannot procure more time. This shows that role overload is also largely dependent on the type of the personality factors that the person possess. Four out of five types of personality i.e. Adjustment, Openness to change, Agreeableness and Conscientiousness were dependent on this factor.

The two most independent factors are Role Stagnation and Role Ambiguity which means that these role stress factors are independent of the personality type the person has. Role Stagnation is when an individual has held on to a role for quite a considerable amount of time, is very comfortably settled, and after that he is asked to take on to a new role, he/she may experience this stress of role stagnation when they are promoted and here the stress caused is irrespective of the personality type of the person. Role Ambiguity is usually experienced when the roles may be newly created and are not well defined. The individual is not clear about the various expectations people have from his role. It may be due to lack of information available or lack of available cues. This stress too is not dependent on the personality type of the individual.

The results also discuss which type of personality is most associated with a particular type of stress factor. The results revealed conscientiousness to be mostly associated with the organisational role stress factors. Eight out of ten times this personality factor is associated with the role stress factors. Thus, a conscientious person is dependent on role stress factors-Inter Role Distance (IRD), Role Expectation Conflict (REC), Role Erosion (RE), Role Overload (RO), Role Isolation (RI), Self-Role Distance (SRD), Role Ambiguity (RA) and Resource Inadequacy (RIn). Conscientiousness refers to efficient/organised vs. easy-going/careless employees of the organisation. A tendency to be organised and dependable, shows self-discipline, act dutifully, aim for achievement, and prefer planned rather spontaneous behaviour. High conscientiousness is often perceived as stubbornness and obsession. Low conscientiousness is associated with flexibility and spontaneity, but can also appear as sloppiness and lack of reliability. Therefore, conscientious person experiences more stress in the organisation.

The least dependency was between the personality type-Agreeableness and the organisational role stress factors. Organisational Role stress factors-Inter Role Distance (IRD), Role Overload (RO) and Role Isolation (RI) had some dependency with the Agreeableness factor that is friendly/compassionate vs. challenging/detached personality of the employees. The other role stress factors were independent to people who fell under the agreeableness dimension of personality.

13

APPLICATION OF RESEARCH

- The personality test used on the workers can also be used by professional firms because, the recruiter can use it to see what strengths and weaknesses are of the employee, and how they match up with the job requirements.
- The combined tests can help the HR of an organisation measure the stress level and personality type, and through that make needed changes in the working curriculum.
- A personality test will provide with an unbiased result for recruiting an individual by processing many attributes present by testing their personality profile.

14

LIMITATIONS OF THE RESEARCH

Methodological limitation

- **Sample size-** As there were only limited workers in the institution for 181 agency, there was a difficulty in finding the relationships from the data. For example, there were less call receivers and more outreach counsellors which hindered the proper representation of the population.

Limitation of the researcher

- **Geographical limitation-** Though the EMRI institution is spread across the country, the data collection was done only from the state of Gujarat. Therefore, the results are a compilation of data collected from women working in 181 agency in Gujarat region.

15

PHOTO GALLERY

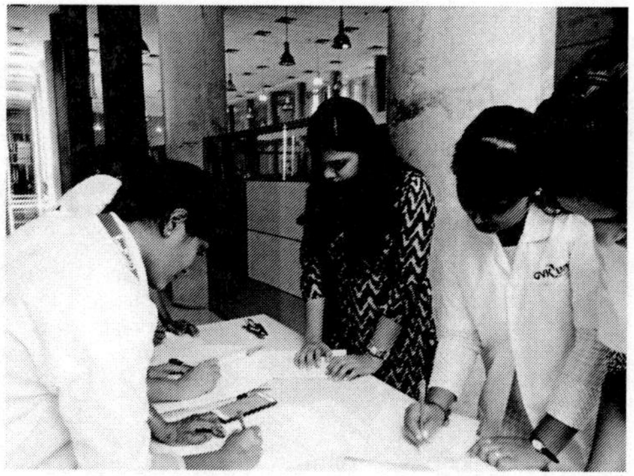

આતાભાઈ ચોકમાં આત્મહત્યા કરતી મહિલાને ૧૮૧ ટીમે બચાવી

ભાવનગર, તા.૭

ભાવનગરમાં કાર્યરત ૧૮૧ મહિના અભયમ હેલ્પલાઈન પરના કાઉન્સેલર ગામીત શિલ્પા દ્વારા તા.૬-૮ રવિવાર સમય ૧૯:૦૨ વાગે સેન્ટર પરથી ફોન આવેલ કે આતાભાઈ ચોકમાં એક અસ્થિર મગજના બહેન રસ્તા વચ્ચે આમથી તેમ દોડે છે અને વાહનો વચ્ચે આવીને આત્મહત્યા કરવાના પ્રવાસો કરે છે. લોકોના પ્રયાસો કરવા છતા તે સમજવા તૈયાર ન હતા.

૧૮૧ ટીમ સહિત તાત્કાલિક ઘટના સ્થળે પહોંચેલ અને બહેન સાથે શાંતિપૂર્વક વાત કરવાની કોશિશ કરેલ. ઘણા સમયના કાઉન્સેલીંગ બાદ તેમણે પોતાનું નામ જણાવ્યું હતું. ઘણા પ્રયત્નો બાદ સુભગ સંસ્થા દ્વારા તેમના કુટુંબીજનોનો નામ-સરનામા મેળવેલ અને તેમનો કોન્ટેકટ કર્યો હતો. ૧૮૧ની ફરજ મુજબ ઈન્દિરાબેન બળવંતરાય વિઠ્ઠલપુરાનો સરનામુ મળી આવતા તેમના ભાઈના દિકરા ફોન કરેલ અને તાત્કાલિક તેમને સહી સલામત તેમના કુટુંબીજનોના ઘરે સોંપી દીધેલ.

પ્રેમ લગ્ન બાદ છૂટાછેડાના દિવસે 181ને ફોન કરી કહ્યું, હું આપઘાત કરવા જઉં છું..

પતિ વિદેશ જવાના મોહમાં કામધંધો કરતા ન હતા અને પત્ની ટ્યુશન કલાસીસ ચલાવતી હતી..

યુવતીના સાસુ છૂટાછેડા બાદ પિયરમાં રહેતા હતા

આણંદમાં HIV ગ્રસ્ત મહિલાને પતિ, ભાઈએ તરછોડતા 181 વાહરે આવી

લાચાર મહિલાને પરિવારે ત્રાસ આપી ઘરમાંથી કાઢી મૂકી હોવાની જાણ થતાં અભયમની ટીમ મદદે પહોંચી હતી

15 વર્ષ પહેલાં પ્રેમી સાથે ભાગેલી મહિલા અંતે પતિ પાસે પાછી ફરી

પ્રેમીનું મૃત્યુ થતાં પતિ પાસે આશરો લેવાની આશા ઠગારી નીવડી

ક્રાઇમરિપોર્ટર | અમદાવાદ

પરિણીતા પ્રેમમાં અંધ થઇ 5 વર્ષની દીકરી અને પતિને છોડી પ્રેમી સાથે ભાગીને લગ્ન કરી લીધા. લગ્નના 15 વર્ષ બાદ બીજા પતિનું મૃત્યુ થતાં તેના પરિવારે પરિણીતાના બન્ને બાળકો રાખી લઇ તેને તગેડી દેતા. 15 વર્ષ પછી પહેલા પતિના ઘરે જઇ આશ્રય આપવા જીદ પર અડી મહિલા હેલ્પલાઇનની મદદ માંગી હતી. મહિલા હેલ્પલાઇનની મદદથી પહેલા પતિ અને દીકરીએ તેને વૃદ્ધાશ્રમમાં રહેવાની વ્યવસ્થા કરી આપી.

બનાસકાંઠાના એક ગામની સીમાનાં લગ્ન અરવલ્લીમાં રહેતા મોહિત નામના એક યુવક સાથે થયા હતાં. બન્નેના લગ્નજીવન દરમિયાન તેઓ એક દીકરીના માતા પિતા બન્યા હતા. સીમા 15 વર્ષ પહેલાં ગાંધીનગરના રોહિત નામના યુવકના પ્રેમમાં પડતા બન્નેએ ભાગીને લગ્ન કરી લીધા હતા.

સીમા 5 વર્ષની દીકરી આસ્થા અને મોહિતને મૂકીને રોહિત સાથે જીવન શરૂ કરી દીધું હતું. રોહિત અને સીમા લગ્નજીવન દરમિયાન 2 સંતાનના માતા પિતા બન્યા હતા. ભાગી ગયાના 15 વર્ષ પછી રોહિતનું મૃત્યુ થતા રોહિતના પરિવારે બન્ને દીકરાઓની કસ્ટડી લઇ સીમાને ઘરમાંથી તગડી દીધી હતી. બાદમાં 15 વર્ષ પછી તે મોહિતના ઘરે જઇને જીદ પર બેસી હતી કે તું મને ફરીથી અપનાવી લે. મોહિત અને દીકરી આસ્થાએ 55 વર્ષીય સીમાને અપનાવવાની ના પાડતા સીમાએ મહિલા હેલ્પલાઇન 181 અભયમની મદદ માંગી હતી. ને કહ્યું હતું કે મારો પતિ અને મારી દીકરી મને ઘરમાં રાખવાની ના પાડે છે.

આ કોલ સાંભળીને 181ના કાઉન્સિલર પ્રીમલબહેન ત્યાં પહોંચ્યા ત્યારે મોહિત અને આસ્થાએ સીમાની હાજરીમાં તે કેવી રીતે આ બન્નેને છોડીને જતી રહી હતી તે અંગે વાત કરી હતી. ત્યારે પ્રીમલે તેમને માનવતાના ધોરણે અન્ય જગ્યાએ રહેવાની વ્યવસ્થા કરી આપવાનું કહેતા મોહિત અને આસ્થાએ તેમને વૃદ્ધાશ્રમમાં મૂકવાનું નક્કી કર્યું. અને સીમાને પોતાની ભૂલ સમજાતા તે વૃદ્ધાશ્રમમાં રહેવાનું સ્વીકારી લીધું હતું.

(પાત્રોના નામ બદલ્યા છે.)

16

PROFILE OF THE RESEARCH TEAM

Project Guide: Dr Neeta Sinha

Dr Neeta Sinha
Assistant Professor
Social Sciences, School of Liberal Studies
neeta.sinha@sls.pdpu.ac.in

Dr. Neeta Sinha is a Behavioural Psychologist, Academician and Corporate Trainer. She holds Ph.D. in the interdisciplinary area of Psychology and Management, Diploma in Mental Retardation. from NIMH Delhi and a Master's degree in Psychology from Patna University. Her teaching, research and industry experience spans over twenty five years. For twelve years she has worked with media industry (The Times of India group) and for the last tweleve years she has been involved in teaching, research, training, psychological counselling and personality development programmes. She is presently working in the Dept. of Psychology, School of Liberal Studies, Pandit Deendayal Petroleum University, Gandhinagar.

Dr. Sinha is very passionate about social issues and has extensively worked with UNICEF and other organisations like 181 Abhayam to look into the challenges prevalent in the society and help mitigate the concerns and be socially productive.

Dr. Sinha is corporate trainer too and her professional experience includes analysis and evaluation of Organisational Behaviour, Organisational Development and other emerging psychological concerns. She has considerable experience and expertise in analyzing and advising corporates and several institutions on their HR policies and conducting training programmes for them. Psychometric assessment, psychological profiling and organisational development are some of her core areas of intervention.

Her professional works include HR Consultancy, business development, key account management; training; design and implementation of selection and development processes; recruitment processes; assessment and development. Stress Management, Emotional Intelligence Gender, Organisational Development, Culture and Environmental concerns are some of the key areas of her interest.

Project Investigator: Miss Simran Bhatia

Simran Bhatia
Psychology and International Relations
School of Liberal Studies (SLS)
Pandit Deendayal Petroleum University (PDPU)
simran.bbb14@sls.pdpu.ac.in

Simran is a very dynamic student and has done various internships, international exposure programmes, research projects, presented various papers in national and international conferences and got them published. Her International Exposure programmes include, IEP to Southern Illinois University, USA and Memoir Writing Essentials at Seattle, Washington, USA. Her Research Projects include: "Multidimensional Vulnerability Assessment of Tribal and Slum Children in Gujarat" by UNICEF, "Women's Economic Empowerment in Asia: Psychosocial and Anthropological Factors" an International Project with Edith Cowan University, Australia, "Civil Society Consultation on State Plan of Action for Children (SPAC)" by UNICEF, "Impact India World Bank 2021" an International Research Project with Fairfield University, USA and Xavier's Research Foundation, and Project titled "Careers in Psychology". She has also presented various papers namely "Study of Organisational Stress experienced by Women employees at Women Helpline Centre in Gujarat" at the 4th International Conference on Stress Management, "Study of Social Intelligence of Liberal Studies and Engineering Students" at the UGC Sponsored National Level Seminar on "Managing Organisational Change for Overall Efficiency", "Cognitive Behavioural Therapy and Depression Management in Type II Diabetic Patients-A Conceptual Study" at the International Conference on Cognitive Behavioural Therapy at All India Institute of Medical Science (AIIMS) etc. She is also the Youth Leader of United for Human Rights Organisation run by United Nations-Universal Declaration of Human Rights and member of Stress Management Association.

Project Investigator: Miss Riddhima Bhatnagar

Riddhima Bhatnagar
Psychology and Human Resource Management
School of Liberal Studies (SLS)
Pandit Deendayal Petroleum University (PDPU)
riddhima.bbb14@sls.pdpu.ac.in

Riddhima is an ambitious student and has done various internships, presented paper at international level, is currently working on the research project which is funded by the college itself. She is also very passionate about Football. Her internships include: working with the "Child Protection Centre" which was in association with UNICEF and a project under the Rajasthan Police Department, she has also completed her internship in Kanoria Hospital and Research Centre from 16th May 2016 to 30th June 2016 completing 60 hours of work in the field of Clinical Psychology. Her research projects include: "Women's Economic Empowerment in Asia: Psychosocial and Anthropological Factors" an International Project with Edith Cowan University, Australia, and "Impact Assessment of Stress Level of Women Working in 181 Abhayam Women Helpline: A Psycho-Social Analysis" a project funded by Pandit Deendayal Petroleum University. She has also presented an International paper on "Styles of Decision Making" at the International Conference of Social Sciences, Literature, Economics and Education at St. Michael's University, University of Toronto, Canada. She has played Football at the National level and has also represented her college in various football tournaments. Currently she is the Captain of her College Football Team.

17

ABBREVIATIONS AND GLOSSARY

1.	EMRI	:	Emergency Management and Research Institute
2.	WHL	:	Women Helpline
3.	OSC	:	One Stop Centre Scheme
4.	PTSD	:	Post-Traumatic Stress Disorder
5.	ORS	:	Organisational Role Stress
6.	IRD	:	Inter Role Distance
7.	RS	:	Role Stagnation
8.	REC	:	Role Expectation Conflict
9.	RE	:	Role Erosion
10.	RO	:	Role Overload
11.	RI	:	Role Isolation
12.	PI	:	Personal Inadequacy
13.	SRD	:	Self-Role Distance

14. RA : Role Ambiguity
15. RIn : Resource Inadequacy
16. A : Adjustment
17. S : Sociability
18. O : Openness to Experience
19. Ag : Agreeableness
20. C : Conscientiousness
21. SPSS : Statistical Package for the Social Sciences
22. DLSA : District Legal Service Authority
23. PO : Protection Officer
24. VAW : Violence Against Women
25. WCD : Women and Child Development
26. UT : Union Territory
27. MWCD : Ministry of Women and Child Development
28. NGO : Non-Governmental Organisation
29. GAS : General Adaptation Syndrome
30. ANOVA : Analysis of Variance

18

REFERENCES

Anon, (2017). [Online] Available at: https://explorable.com/what-is-stress?gid=1600

Apa.org. (2017). [Online] Available at: http://www.apa.org/helpcentre/workplace-stress.aspx

Ccohs.ca. (2017). Workplace Stress - General: OSH Answers. [Online] Available at: http://www.ccohs.ca/oshanswers/psychosocial/stress.html

Bowie, B. (1966). The High School Journal, 50(2), 103-104. Retrieved from http://www.jstor.org/stable/40366364

Burton, J., Hoobler, J., and Scheuer, M. (2012). Supervisor Workplace Stress and Abusive Supervision: The Buffering Effect of Exercise. Journal of Business and Psychology, 27(3), 271-279. Retrieved from http://www.jstor.org/stable/41682913

Charlton, B. (1992). Stress. Journal of Medical Ethics, 18(3), 156-159. Retrieved from http://www.jstor.org/stable/27717198

Dolan, S., Van Ameringen, M., and Arsenault, A. (1992). Personality, Social Support and Workers' Stress. Relations Industrielles / Industrial Relations, 47(1), 125-139. Retrieved from http://www.jstor.org/stable/23073812

En.wikipedia.org. (2017). Occupational stress. [Online] Available at: https://en.wikipedia.org/wiki/Occupational_stress.

Gilbert, R. (1985). Personality, Stress and Achievement: Keys to Presidential Longevity. Presidential Studies Quarterly, 15(1), 33-50. Retrieved from http://www.jstor.org/stable/27550163

Gustems-Carnicer, J., and Calderón, C. (2013). Coping strategies and psychological well-being among teacher education students: Coping and well-being in students. European Journal of Psychology of Education, 28(4), 1127-1140. Retrieved from http://www.jstor.org/stable/23580901

Grcgujarat.org. (2017). Gender Resource Centre- Women and child development Institute – Ahmedabad Gujarat India. [Online] Available at: http://www.grcgujarat.org/advice-rescue-counselling.html

indiainfoline.com. (2017). GVK EMRI launches "Abhayam"–Women Helpline 181 in the State of Gujarat. [Online] Available at: http://www.indiainfoline.com/article/news-sector-telecom/gvk-emri-launches-abhayam—women-helpline-181-in-the-state-of-gujarat-114021000056_1.html

J. S. Pandya, P., Speaks, G., Pandya, P., Patel, K., Pandya, P., Patel, B., Patel, B., Patel, B., Pandya, P., J, S., Patel, K., Patel, A. Agarkar, F. Patel, A. and Patel, K. (2017). Gujarat Government's 'Abhayam' Women Helpline Launched. [Online] Womenpla.net. Available at: http://womenpla.net/gujarat-governments-abhayam-women-helpline-launched/

Jstor.org. (2017). Psychological Stress on JSTOR. [Online] Available at: https://www.jstor.org/topic/psychological-stress/?refreqid=search%3A54651135ceba9f10025a98c19dd33799

Kulkarni, P. and Deoras, N. (2017). Why employees in India are stressed at workplaces. [Online] The Economic Times. Available at: http://economictimes.indiatimes.com/magazines/panache/why-employees-in-india-are-stressed-at-workplaces/articleshow/47655329.cms

Latack, J., and Havlovic, S. (1992). Coping with Job Stress: A Conceptual Evaluation Framework for Coping Measures. Journal of Organisational Behavior, 13(5), 479-508. Retrieved from http://www.jstor.org/stable/2488399

Osborne, H. (2017). Psychometric tests in job interviews: what are they looking for? [Online] the Guardian. Available at: https://www.theguardian.com/money/shortcuts/2014/jan/29/psychometric-tests-job-interviews-what-for

Rai, S., and Kumar, V. (2012). Five Factor Model of Personality and Role Stress. Indian Journal of Industrial Relations, 48(2), 341-353. Retrieved from http://www.jstor.org/stable/23509843

Sethi, A. (1982). Stress Coping. Canadian Journal of Public Health / Revue Canadienne De Sante'e Publique, 73(4), 267-271. Retrieved from http://www.jstor.org/stable/41994236

Sidle, S. (2008). Workplace Stress Management Interventions: What Works Best? Academy of Management Perspectives, 22(3), 111-112. Retrieved from http://www.jstor.org/stable/27747467

Spector, P. (2002). Employee Control and Occupational Stress. Current Directions in Psychological Science, 11(4), 133-136. Retrieved from http://www.jstor.org/stable/20182790

Topper, E. (2003). Working Knowledge: Dealing with Workplace Stress. American Libraries, 34(2), 62-62. Retrieved from http://www.jstor.org/stable/256486

19

ANNEXURE

QUESTIONNAIRE - I

ORCP 131

મોટા પાંચ સૂચક પ્રશ્નાવલિ

સૂચના: દરેક આંકડાકીય સ્કેલ પર, જે સંખ્યા તમને સામાન્ય રીતે વધુ વર્ણનાત્મક લાગે, તે પસંદ કરો. જો બંને શબ્દો સમાન રીતે વર્ણનાત્મક હોય તો, મિડપોઈન્ટને ચિહ્નિત કરો.

તારીખ: નામ: ઉંમર:

જાતિ: સંસ્થા: અનુભવના વર્ષ:

1	આતુર	5	4	3	2	1	શાંત
2	અન્ય લોકો સાથે ગમે	5	4	3	2	1	એકલા રહેવું પસંદ છે
3	સ્વપ્નદ્રષ્ટા	5	4	3	2	1	વાસ્તવિક
4	નમ્ર	5	4	3	2	1	અસભ્ય
5	સુઘડ	5	4	3	2	1	અવ્યવસ્થિત

6	સાવચેત	5	4	3	2	1	સ્વખાતરી
7	આશાવાદી	5	4	3	2	1	નિરાશાવાદી
8	અનુમાનિત	5	4	3	2	1	વ્યવહારુ
9	ઉદાર	5	4	3	2	1	સ્વાર્થી
10	નિર્ણાયક	5	4	3	2	1	ઉદારવાદી

11	નિરાશા	5	4	3	2	1	પ્રસન્નતા
12	દેખાડો	5	4	3	2	1	વ્યક્તિગત
13	કલ્પના અનુસાર	5	4	3	2	1	અન્ના અનુસાર
14	પ્રેમાળ	5	4	3	2	1	અસભ્ય
15	ધ્યાન કેન્દ્રિત	5	4	3	2	1	સરળતાથી વિચલિત

16	સરળતાથી બેચેની	5	4	3	2	1	ધ્યાન ન આપવી
17	મૈત્રીપૂર્ણ	5	4	3	2	1	ક્રૂર
18	નવીનતા શોધવી	5	4	3	2	1	સમાનતા લેવી
19	આધારિત	5	4	3	2	1	સ્વતંત્ર
20	સંપૂર્ણતા માટે પસંદગી	5	4	3	2	1	અવ્યવસ્થિત આદત

21	નિયંત્રિત વ્યક્તિ	5	4	3	2	1	શાંત વ્યક્તિ
22	બોલકું માણસ	5	4	3	2	1	વિચારશીલ વ્યક્તિ
23	અનિશ્ચિતતા સાથે આરામ	5	4	3	2	1	સ્પષ્ટ વસ્તુઓની પસંદગી
24	વિશ્વાસનીય વ્યક્ત	5	4	3	2	1	શંકાસ્પદ
25	સમય અનુસાર	5	4	3	2	1	વિલંબ કરવું

આભાર.

QUESTIONNAIRE II

<u>ઓઆરએસ સ્કેલ</u>

આ પ્રશ્નાવલી એ કામના સ્થળે અનુભવાતું માનસિક દબાણ કે જે તમે કર્મચારી તરીકે તમારી ભૂમિકા ભજવવાનો અનુભવ કરો છો.
અહીં ૫૦ પ્રશ્નો છે. મહેરબાની કરી નિવેદનને તપાસો અને તમને કેટલી વાર આ વિધાન પરત્વે લાગણી વ્યક્ત થાય છે. તમારી લાગણીના આધારે દરેક નિવેદનને રેટિંગ આપો.

લખો: 0 જો તમે ભાગ્યે જ અથવા ક્યારેય આ અનુભવતા નથી.

1 જો તમે ક્યારેક ક્યારેક (થોડા સમય માટે) આ અનુભવું છું.

2 જો કોઈક વખત આ અનુભવું છું.

3 જો હું વારંવાર આ અનુભવું છું.

4 જો હું વારંવાર અથવા કાયમ આ અનુભવું છું.

નોંધ : જો તમને લાગે કે તમારી લાગણી જે કેટેગરીમાં વ્યક્ત થાય છે તે બરોબર નથી તો તેને નજીકનું જે અનુભવાય તે જણાવો. મહેરબાની કરીને કોઈ મુદ્દો જવાબ વગરનો છોડશો નહિ.

નામ : ____________________ ઉંમર : __________

જાતિ(M/F) : __________

સંસ્થા : ____________________

અનુભવના વર્ષ : ____________________

અ. નુ. નં.	વિધાન	ક્યારેય નહિ કે દુર્લભ રીતે આ અનુભવ્યું હોય તો (0)	પ્રસંગોપાત આ રીતે અનુભવ્યું હોય તો (1)	ક્યારેક આ રીતે અનુભવ્યું હોય તો (2)	વારંવાર આ રીતે અનુભવ્યું હોય તો (3)	વારંવાર કે હંમેશ આ રીતે અનુભવ્યું હોય તો (4)
1	મારી ભૂમિકા (કામ) મારી વ્યક્તિગત જીંદગીમાં દખલ કરે છે.					
2	મને બીક છે કે હું મારી હાલની પ્રોફાઈલમાં ઉચ્ચ જવાબદારી લેવા માટે પુરતું શીખતો નથી.					
3	હું મારી આસપાસના પરસ્પર વિરોધી માંગ ધરાવતા લોકોને પુરતો સંતોષ આપી શકતો નથી.					
4	મારી ભૂમિકા મને પુરતું મહત્વ અપાવી શકતી નથી.					
5	મારો કાર્યભાર ખુબ વધારે છે.					
6	અન્ય લોકો મને પુરતું મહત્વ અને સમય આપતા નથી.					
7	મારી ભૂમિકા નિભાવવા માટે જરૂરી એવું પુરતું જ્ઞાન મારી પાસે નથી.					
8	મારે એવા કામ કરવા પડે છે જે મારા વધુ સારા નિર્ણયથી ઉલટા હોય.					
9	મારી શૈક્ષણિક અને ઈતર અભ્યાસેત્તર પ્રવૃત્તિઓની ભૂમિકા મારા ક્ષેત્ર અને જવાબદારીઓની કામગીરીમાં શું છે તે બાબતે હું સ્પષ્ટ નથી.					
10	મને જે કામ સોપવામાં આવ્યું છે તે પૂર્ણ કરવા જરૂરી માહિતી મને પ્રાપ્ત થતી નથી.					
11	મને બીજા ઘણાં રસ છે (સામાજિક, ધાર્મિક વગેરે) જેને અવગણું છે કારણ કે મને તે માટે પુરતો સમય મળતો નથી.					

12	અન્ય જવાબદારીઓની લેવાની તૈયારી માટે હું મારી હાલની જવાબદારીઓમાં ખુબ રોકાયેલો છું.					
13	હું અનેકવિધ પ્રકૃતિવાળા લોકો અને સીનીયરની વિરોધાભાસી માંગ સંતોષી શકુ તેમ નથી.					
14	ઘણાં કામ જે મારી ભૂમિકા (કામ)નો એક ભાગ છે તે બીજા અન્ય કોઈને સોંપવામાં આવ્યા છે. (મને જેવું જોઈએ તેવું ખુલ્લાપણું મળતું નથી.)					
15	કામની માત્રા જે મારે કરવી પડે છે તે હું જે ગુણવત્તા જાળવવા માંગું છું તેમાં દખલ કરે છે.					
16	સંસ્થામાં મારા કામ અને અન્ય કામ વચ્ચે પુરતા પ્રમાણમાં ક્રિયાપ્રતિક્રિયા થતી નથી.					
17	હું એવું ઈચ્છું છું કે મને જે કામ સોપવામાં આવે છે તે માટે મારી પાસે વધુ કૌશલ્ય હોય.					
18	મારા અગાઉના જ્ઞાન/ટ્રેનીંગ અને કુશળતાનો ઉપયોગ હું અત્યારના કામમાં કરી શકવા સમર્થ નથી.					
19	મને ખબર નથી કે જે લોકો સાથે હું કામ કરું છું તે મારી પાસે શું ઈચ્છે છે.					
20	મને મારા કામમાં અસરકારક બનવા માટે યોગ્ય સંશાધનો મળતા નથી.					
21	મારું કામ મને મારા પરિવાર/મિત્રો માટે પુરતો સમય ફાળવવા મંજુરી આપતું નથી.					
22	મારા કામ અંગેના ભવિષ્યના સૂચિત પડકારો માટે મારી જાતને તૈયાર કરવા મારી પાસે સમય અને તક નથી.					
23	હું સંસ્થામાં મારી આસપાસના લોકોની માંગને					
	સંતોષી શકતો નથી કેમ કે તેઓ પરસ્પર વિરોધાભાસી છે.					
24	મને અત્યાર છે તેના કરતા વધારે જવાબદારી લેવાનું પસંદ છે.					
25	મને ખૂબ વધારે જવાબદારી સોપવામાં આવી છે.					
26	ગુણવત્તા સુધારવા માટેની જૂથ પ્રવૃત્તિઓ દ્વારા મને આશા છે કે મારા અને અન્યોના કામ અંગે વધારે પરામર્શ મળે.					
27	મેં મારી ભૂમિકા (કામ) સાથે સંબંધિત તૈયારી અને તાલીમ હજી લીધી નથી.					
28	જે કોર્સ હાથ ધર્યો છે તે મારા રસ સાથે સંકળાયેલો નથી.					
29	મારા કામના ઘણા બધા પાસા અને જવાબદારીઓ પ્રસંગોપાત ધૂંધળા અને અસ્પષ્ટ છે.					
30	મારી ભૂમિકા (જવાબદારી) પૂરી પાડવા કામ કરવા મારી પાસે પુરતા લોકો નથી.					
31	મારી હાલની જવાબદારીઓ મારે જે પ્રવૃત્તિઓ કરવી છે તેમાં દખલ કરે છે.					
32	મેં જે કોર્સ પસંદ કર્યો છે તેમાં વ્યક્તિગત વિકાસને ઘણો ઓછો અવકાશ છે.					
33	હું મારા સિનિયર અને જુનીયર તથા સમવયસ્ક પાસેથી વિરોધાભાસી માંગણીઓ મેળવું છું.					
34	જેટલું મને સોંપાયું છે તેનાથી હું ઘણું વધારે કરી શકું છું.					
35	મારા કાર્યભારને થોડો ઓછો કરવાની જરૂરિયાત					

	છે.					
36	એવા કોઈ પુરાવા નથી કે ઘણી બધી ભૂમિકાઓ (મારી ભૂમિકા સહિત)નો સમાવેશ કોઈ એક સહિયારી સમસ્યાનું નિરાકરણ કરવા કે સંયુક્ત આયોજન કરવા થાય.					
37	હું ઈચ્છું છું કે મેં મારી જાતને હાલના કામ અંગે સારી રીતે તૈયાર કરી હોત.					
38	જો મારા કામને વ્યાખ્યાયિત કરવામાં મને પૂર્ણ સ્વાતંત્ર્ય હોત તો હું અત્યારે જે રીતે કામ કરી રહ્યો છું તેના કરતા કંઈક જુદી રીતે કરતો હોત.					
39	મારે કયા પ્રકારની જવાબદારીઓ નિભાવવાની છે તે બાબતે હું વધારે સ્પષ્ટ નથી.					
40	હું કેટલાક અંશે ચિંતાગ્રસ્ત છું કે હું મારી ભૂમિકા (કામ) માટે જરૂરી અનુકુળતા ધરાવતો નથી.					
41	મારા કામની સૂચી અનુસાર ભારે કામને કારણે મારી પરિવાર અને મિત્રો ફરીયાદ કરે છે કે હું તેમની સાથે સમય પસાર કરતો/કરી શકતો નથી.					
42	હું એવું અનુભવું છું કે મારા કામમાં પુરતો બૌદ્ધિક વિકાસ નથી.					
43	વિવિધ લોકોની મારી ભૂમિકા (કામ) અંગેની પરસ્પર વિરોધાભાસી અપેક્ષાઓ અંગે હું હેરાન છું.					
44	હું ઈચ્છું છું કે મને વધારે પડકારરૂપ કાર્ય કરવા મળે.					
45	હું મારી ભૂમિકા (કામ) અંગે વધુ પડતો બોજો અનુભવું છું.					
46	હું ચર્ચા કે મદદ કરવા પહેલ કરું ત્યારે પણ મને આસપાસના અન્ય લોકો પાસેથી યોગ્ય					
	પ્રતિસાદ મળતો નથી.					
47	મારા કામમાં કાર્યક્ષમ બનવા માટે મને વધારે તાલીમ અને તૈયારીની જરૂર છે.					
48	હું મારા મૂલ્યો અને મને સોંપેલુ કામ જે હું કરું છું તેમાં સંઘર્ષ અનુભવું છું.					
49	મારી ભૂમિકામાં રહેલી પ્રાથમિકતા બાબતે હું વધારે સ્પષ્ટ નથી.					
50	મને સોંપવામાં આવેલા કામ અંગે હું ઈચ્છું છું કે મારી પાસે વધારે સારા (નાણાકીય/વસ્તુ) સંશાધનો હોય.					